The Incredible Investment Book

The Incredible Investment Book

By

Charles G. Salisbury

New York

The Incredible Investment Book
The #1 Way to Invest in the #1 Investment in America

ISBN 978-1-60037-664-1

Library of Congress Control Number: 2009929287

MORGAN · JAMES
THE ENTREPRENEURIAL PUBLISHER

Morgan James Publishing, LLC
1225 Franklin Ave., STE 325
Garden City, NY 11530-1693
Toll Free 800-485-4943
www.MorganJamesPublishing.com

In an effort to support local communities, raise awareness and funds, Morgan James Publishing donates one percent of all book sales for the life of each book to Habitat for Humanity. Get involved today, visit **www.HelpHabitatForHumanity.org.**

You Are What You Think

If you think you are beaten, you are,
If you think that you dare not, you don't
If you'd like to win, but you think you can't,
It's almost certain you won't.
If you think you'll lose, you've lost,
For out in the world you'll find
Success begins with a fellows will –
It's all in the state of mind.
If you think you are outclassed, you are;
You've got to think high to rise;
You've got to be sure of yourself before
You can ever win the prize.
Life's battles don't always go
To the stronger or fastest man;
But soon or late the man who wins
Is the man who thinks he **can**.

Chuck Salisbury

Contents

Foreword

Every author has someone to thank and I am no exception. Just writing the book itself is a great relief for the soul and a generous benefit to the reader if the contents have any redeeming value. Whether a fiction or non fiction, biography or fantasy, behind every author is the inspiration that leads them to think that they actually have something of value to offer to the public. My inspiration is faith based and family based. For starters I am a Christian who has been tested through good times and devastating times. It's easy to be faithful during good times but it's difficult to be loyal to your faith when it seems that God is punishing you for some casual or serious misdeed. Having been blessed to the maximum and then not being grateful by being a poor steward is a test of one's faith. When you loose it all, you appreciate God's many blessings and makes you realize that it's not yours after all. Few Christians have had that fact driven home so completely as I have. I can now separate between material "things" and lasting permanent blessings represented by family, friends and good health. A client of mine said it this way...

"Your Health is Your Wealth". He realized that fact because he was very wealthy but had lost his health and couldn't buy it back.

I want to say that my blessings are my family and the many friends that are a part of my life. My children have always been a priority and are God's greatest blessing. My Mom (Eva Salisbury) is still active at age 90 and has provided love, support and lots of hugs since my birth. As a "stay at home Mom" she provided the example of determination and tough love along with tempered criticism when necessary. She saw to it that her children attended Sunday School every Sunday and eventually encouraged Dad to attend Church with her every week. Thanks for being such a blessing Mom. My sister inherited Mom's determination which has encouraged her to also be a positive example for me and for her family. Thanks Carol (little Sis) for being such a special sister. My younger brother Les was a great golfer and runner at Morton High School in Morton, Ill. I used to love watching him run relays as he had great speed and form.

My son Christopher, age 12, is a blessing beyond compare. As a straight A student and an outstanding Football and Basketball player, I recognize that someday I will be remembered as Chris' Dad. His dream of becoming an NFL Quarterback will be realized because he is always serious about his goals and very determined to achieve them. I look forward to the day when he takes the field and leads an NFL team to victory. He brought people into my life to remind me of His other numerous blessings.

Friends are a positive influence and mine are numerous. My special friends are Stan Marshall whose friendship goes all the way back to Woodruff High School in Peoria, Ill. I used to work as a Branch Manager for Jack Hereth in the early 80's and we remain strong Christian Brothers. Jack and his wife Dawn will always be a shinning example of what can be achieved if you remain faithful to each other and live by Christian standards without exception. Their large family is amazing because they are amazing. My local and very special friend is Bennie Lagos whose Christian love and commitment to high standards of faith and forgiveness is a standard for others to follow. As a member and minister at Saddleback Church he created the Pacific Islanders ministry and shares his love with hundreds of people every week. When I need a boast or a prayer Bennie is always there for me. For the hundreds of other friends, not mentioned here, I share the words of Dr. Robert Schuller who says "God Loves You and So Do I".

This book is full of positive influence tempered by 40 years of investment experience. I know that the investment real estate investment advice contained within the Chapters of this book can be appreciated far more by those that have experienced some failure while investing in real estate. There are many Guru's who sponsor seminars focusing on various ways to buy real estate. Most of these seminars attract people through the use of large newspaper ads, radio and T.V. spots. I have been to many of them and, through time, have noticed that the seminars are really created to sell books, tapes and other instructional courses costing hundreds if not thousands of dollars. Some focus on Foreclosures, Probate Sales, Flipping Property, etc. Very few people make any money following the advice of these seminar leaders. They are interesting and sometimes motivating but are usually only profitable for the sponsors. I therefore suggest that everyone remember this practical advice...Buyer Beware.

Finally, I want to thank you for buying this book and making a financial investment in your future. This book is only the beginning not the end. The journey towards financial independence can be short or last a lifetime. Some of you will be inspired to register at my website www.TenPercentDown.com and go on to attend one of my Free Seminars, take a tour of selected areas of the U.S. where we are buying property and getting involved in learning all you can about every aspect of my investment program. Others will enjoy a short trip of enlightenment and inspiration with little follow-through. Your life, by choice, will not change and your future will be as it was before. I'm sorry for you as you can be identified as a dreamer and not a doer.

It's the doers who will make a difference in their life and in the life of their children and grandchildren. They will retire with dignity and enough financial resources. The doers will travel, enjoy free time with family and friends, support their church and leave an estate to their family and favorite charities. Since life is about daily choices I hope that every reader will choose to be a Doer and enjoy the many blessings that God has provided. Don't just watch...participate. I want your life to be blessed and I share my life experiences and positive conclusions so that you don't have to spend 40 years learning how to invest correctly. This book is a passport to financial freedom. But having a passport without booking the trip is a terrible waste. Decide today to take the trip to financial security.

The Introduction

The most successful investment in the United States is not stocks, bonds, mutual funds, commodities, annuities or any related products. The best investment is Real Estate and this book outlines the best way to invest in income property. There isn't a better investment in America today and you will learn why by reading this informative book.

The interest in real estate investment has never been higher. More seminars, books, tapes and promotions on radio, T.V. and newspapers validates the public's realization that real estate is the number one way to build wealth in America and there isn't a close second. However, many books, tapes and seminars are a rehash of old ideas that create great copy and promise riches but most are out of touch with today's market. People following these old useless ideas will not enjoy the positive experience and growth available by knowing what to do today and why.

Chuck Salisbury, the author, has been buying property for over 40 years and attended many of these seminars, bought the books and tapes and followed the advice of most of today's real estate guru's. He was also a stockbroker (1974 – 1996) with major Wall Street firms for 22 years and as a successful broker purchased real estate primarily as a tax shelter. Despite the tax benefits, he didn't approach real estate as a serious investment until he finally figured out his current formula. As a result, he is building an estate very quickly and enjoying a ROI far beyond anything he was able to offer to investors while he was a stock broker. His radio show and seminars attract hundreds of admirers who want a secure future and retirement with dignity. Chuck delivers what many others promise. The Incredible Investment Book will change the way people invest in Real Estate forever. Don't invest in **anything** until you've read his book.

Chapter 1

The Incredible Investment Book

The Quick Fix for Get Rich

The Incredible Investment Book is more than a primer. This is a fact-based summary of the very best way to build a substantial net worth within your lifetime. Yes, you can retire with dignity, and the results begin when you start applying the principles presented by this book—as soon as one hour from now. That's how long it takes to read this book.

You can attend seminars for the next 10 years and come to the same conclusion that I'm presenting to you today. I know. I attended many "investment clinics" and then followed much of their gurus' advice. I also presented seminars on fixed-income securities, which represent a conservative approach to building wealth. This book is a summary of THE best way to invest your money and earn 100% per year with less risk than stocks, bonds, mutual funds or variable annuities.

Despite the excitement that you'll feel when you complete this book, there's still one very important factor that could keep you from enjoying any of the benefits presented in this book. I've found that the biggest handicap facing the thousands of people who have attended my seminars, heard my radio program and seen me on TV is this: Most people are procrastinators. No matter how powerful my message is or how motivated people are, there's a natural tendency to "think about it" or "talk to someone else." Quite frankly, most people aren't doers…they're thinkers. I like people to think, to ask questions, get opinions and work toward the goal of making a decision. But after you've done all your due diligence and know everything there is to know, can you actually make a decision? Many people can't and are afraid to do anything serious to change their life. Therefore, their life doesn't change. They'll keep doing what they've always done and get the results they've always gotten because it's comfortable. I like to describe procrastination this way… "It's failure before you ever begin." You can never experience success without stepping out and taking a chance even if the results are sometimes a failure. I remember my Dad saying, "You can't win unless you play the game." He also said that failure is still a lesson learned, so that you'll know better next time.

The advice in this book is a summary of more than 35 years of personal experience, and I'm sharing only the results that have consistently worked year after year. This counsel will continue to work for the rest of your life and your children's lives. I want to help you build an estate to take care of you, your children and your grandchildren. This book will enable you to do that and more. Only your procrastination can prevent you from succeeding and prospering. Please think about that before you read any further. Have you decided to be a doer or a dreamer? You purchased this book, which is the act of a doer. Don't let anyone or anything stop you from taking the advice I offer and following it exactly. If you do that, you'll get the best possible results. Don't change the rules or make exceptions, because everything is written for a specific purpose. This book will only be "Incredible" if you are ready to become "Incredible" with the advice it presents. Don't let others tell you it doesn't work or that they have a better plan. They don't, and it does work 100% of the time. Are you ready for a life-changing experience? Then let's move on to the best way to build wealth.

This book is dedicated to every person who has a retirement account and expects his or her investment to grow at a reasonable rate so that he or she will have enough money to retire comfortably. It's also written for the millions of homeowners who have built equity in their home as a result of appreciation through inflation. The unfortunate conclusion is that few people will actually enjoy the benefits of financial independence when they retire. The reason is no mystery, and all investors should know the truth and accept it so they can make adjustments in their investment strategy. First, you need to accept the fact that there are two basic money principles and that understanding them will impact every investment decision you make from this date forward. Please understand that there is YOUR money and OPM (other people's money), and the best money to invest is OPM. The second principle is to never invest in anything that doesn't adjust for inflation. Let's go into more detail about the OPM principle so you'll know which side of the fence you're on. You've heard the expression that the "grass is greener on the other side of the fence." In the case of basic money/investment principles, it's actually a true statement. As you stand on your side of the fence, you have your money and you invest it yourself with the help of facilitators such as stock brokerage firms, insurance companies and banks. These three are located on the other side of the fence, and they all make their money using OPM, which means they make money with your money. During my 22-year career as a stockbroker, I always understood that my primary responsibility was to be a magnet to attract money from various investors. The amount of money under management translated into the amount of income I earned and the amount of money that the brokerage firm made.

I was rewarded year after year based upon my production, not the success of my clients. As a member of the "Chairman's Council," I was rewarded with a impressive plaque and a trip to an annual banquet at some five-star resort destination. I was offered other incentives as well, such as trips and gifts, to encourage the sale of certain company-sponsored products. Putting clients into partnerships and mutual funds created by the firm was good business for the brokers and for the firm but not so good for the clients. Stockbrokers were selected because of their sales skills, not their technical skills. The same can be said about financial advisers, financial planners and registered investment advisers. They all make a living based upon the commissions they create, which requires that they sell products. Most brokers depend on the sales material, research reports and summary packages created by the firms they represent. Most also understand that they begin every month with a zero balance in the commission account, so they have to review their customer accounts to determine the best ways to create sales activity and, of course, earn that paycheck by month's end.

A few firms have redefined their compensation schedule so that it appears they're paying salaries. Consequently, there's no compelling incentive to create sales. Still, these new compensation schedules don't eliminate the challenge to create sales. Why? Because the rewards are still based upon production, and the responsibility to "attract capital" is still very strong. All the best perks still go to those who attract the most new capital and create the most commission sales. The least qualified of all "financial advisers" are those employed by banks. They're a step above tellers and know little about investments except what they've been taught. The teaching, however, is self-serving because, as a rule, banks offer limited investment options.

It's my strong belief that the ideal compensation schedule should be directly tied to successful results for clients. For example, a broker could be compensated on a percentage of the profits created by the broker and the firm for which he or she works. Sounds good, but don't expect that to happen. The growth and success of stock brokerage firms depends on the amount of OPM they have under management. They're on the right side of the fence, and you're on the wrong side. They make money with your money whether or not you make a profit. They can't lose because it's your money, not theirs.

What about banks? You can deposit money in a savings account and feel comfortable because it's protected by FDIC insurance. Certificates of deposit (CDs) are another choice. Many banks have also found that they can increase their profitability by offering brokerage instruments such as mutual funds and insurance products. But buying investment products from a bank offers no more security than buying them from a stock brokerage firm. Overall, mutual funds are a failure for the investors and a profitable windfall for the brokerage firms as well as banks. Read the Chapter on Mutual Funds in this book.

Even though they're purchased at a bank, there's no FDIC protection for investment products. Banks offer various investment products to increase their own profits. Banks skillfully explain that they offer investment products so they can be a "full service" and "one stop" source for all your investment needs.

It's nice to know that banks now allow you to lose money with them so you don't have to continue losing your money only with stock brokerage firms! Seems the banks want to provide an equal opportunity to create losses for their clients so they can increase their profitability. Again, using OPM is the right side of the fence for them as well as the stock brokerage firms.

Banks make money by attracting money, paying interest on your money, and lending it back to you and others at a higher rate. Want to buy a house or a car? Then you get a loan from your bank, savings and loan or credit union. Without your money and the ability to leverage that money through the Federal Government, they simply can't do business. Banks not only make money through lending and various investment products; they also own their own real estate. Have you noticed that banks have prime locations and new buildings from which to operate? Yes, it's your money being invested in real estate to create a financially healthy banking business.

Do you wonder how insurance companies can pay those sizable death benefits to a policy owner? If you buy a term life insurance policy and then pay the insurance company monthly for many years, the payment doesn't get placed in a savings account in your name. The money goes to the insurance company, which invests your money along with all the other policy payments. The insurance company doesn't put your money in a passbook account, a CD or mutual fund. The company invests it in real estate and also lends construction money to builders of large projects. Insurance companies create profits using OPM; they're on the right side of the fence. They understand that their real business is creating products that attract more money from the public and generate opportunities for them to continue investing OPM in various profitable ventures. The insurance companies have even gotten involved in mutual funds through offering variable annuities that require an investment in products that have risks and provide further opportunities to lose your money.

Every year the investment public is trying to keep ahead of the loss curve by trusting key decisions to people who work for the big three: stock brokerage firms, banks and savings and loans, and insurance companies. All three sectors hire people to sell products to the public, and those employees receive compensation and bonuses according to their ability to attract more OPM to keep their respective companies in the black. None of them reward their employees based upon how well they treat their clients or how successfully they invest your money and create profits for you. Their staff members get the same pay whether you make money or lose money. There's no incentive to make money for you at the expense of their own company's profitability. Knowing that should bring a powerful sense of accountability to your own investment decisions from this day forward.

You must take charge of your own investments if you want to grow your accounts so you can retire with dignity. This book will present a clear path to what we believe is a simple but very disciplined approach to real estate investments—an approach that will generate very positive results through the use of other peoples money (OPM) and put YOU on the right side of the fence. Then you can make money for yourself and your family. You can break your dependence on the BIG three and set a certain course toward financial security and success!

Chapter 2

Investigating the Investments

What Works and What Doesn't

In this chapter I'll present the facts about different popular investments from 1960 through 2006, to give you a clear and honest "frame of reference." This information will be especially valuable if others start to question the wisdom of investing all your money in real estate. When they ask, you can confidently reply that, evaluated by return on investment (ROI), real estate has been and continues to be the best investment in the United States. There's not even a close second!

"But what about diversification?" your abandoned stock broker or financial adviser quizzes. Then you can confidently answer: "I own property in North and South Carolina, Texas, Oklahoma and Nebraska. How diversified do you want me to be?"

Let me share a few thoughts from my seminars that I feel are important to mention here. First, celebrated American humorist Will Rogers gave this tongue-in-cheek summary of his investment criteria: "I'm not so concerned about the return **ON** my investment as the return

OF my investment." I also like to quote baseball great Yogi Berra, who said. "It ain't braggin' if you can do it."

For obvious reasons, I refer to Yogi's comment when I tell prospective clients that I've consistently enjoyed a 100% ROI since I started using my strict real estate investment formula. If you do what I do, you'll definitely experience the same highly profitable results.

Because I spent 22 years as a stock broker and investment banker, I know a few things about traditional investments offered by stock brokerage firms. Thanks to that extensive experience, I'm able to share the truth and let investors decide.

When people ask what I think of the "securities" in their portfolio, I tell them such investments lead to "insecurities" because the stock market is anything but secure. No one in the world knows how the market will do the next day, the next week, month or year. How can that lead to financial security? Can you build a comfortable retirement by investing in unstable, unpredictable and questionable securities? Possibly—but not likely! You'll definitely be taking your chances. And one thing that stocks, bonds and money (currency) have in common is that they continue to print more of them daily. What does that tell you?

OK, ask me about investing in commodities, and I'll respond that they're *not* an investment. Commodities fall into the same category as slot machines, card games and roulette. Go to Las Vegas, have some fun and *expect to lose*. The commodities business is filed with salespeople whose only business is to convince you that they possess superior knowledge about the future of gold, silver, oil and the like. Give me a break!

I recall a story about a certain "investor" who was asked what attracted him to commodities. He replied, "Well, there's a lot of money to be made in that market." Then he was asked, "How do you know?" His answer: "Because I put a lot of money in it myself."

The worst thing that can happen is that you do a trade and actually make some money. As happens with many gamblers, you'll probably view this as evidence that you've discovered the road to riches. You'll come to believe that you can "figure it out" and get rich.

Typically, even when you start losing money (everyone does), you'll then keep pouring money into new strategies. It's kind of like continuing to buy lottery tickets despite the fact that you've purchased them for years and never won. Incredibly, some poor folks actually believe that their retirement account consists of winning the lottery. The same type of naïve thinking is behind commodity investing.

Sorry to burst your bubble, but in the long run—and more often than not, the short run too—the house always wins. As long as the commodities firms continue spending big bucks on advertising, they'll continue to find new victims and separate them from their money. These firms make money on every trade whether you do or not, and they're constantly on the prowl for new money.

Let's continue with my summary of popular investment options so you can compare them to real estate. Next up. . .bonds. What can be wrong with bonds? First, you must understand the effect of inflation on your bond portfolio. In the absence of inflation, there'd be no problem. But inflation figures from 1960 to the present (*see illustration*) reveal that, in one form or another, inflation is here to stay.

Here's a real-life experience that should convince you that bonds are, in fact, a *depreciable asset.* In 1975 I was working in Beverly Hills for a firm called Stern Brenner & Co. We specialized in municipal bonds, and I developed a very credible client list by conducting seminars for wealthy people and their accountants. As a result, I sold a lot of "muni" bonds in large numbers.

One instructive "for instance": I sold $100,000 of California General Obligation bonds with a 30-year maturity paying 5% tax free to an investor. I also bought my first home in Valencia, California, in 1975 for $48,500. It was a four-bedroom, three-bath, 2,000+-sq.-ft. residence purchased with the help of my VA benefits.

Fast forward 30 years and consider the results. Today that home is worth about $750,000. The bonds, on the other hand, just matured, and the investor got his $100,000 back. But what can you buy with $100,000 today versus 1975? That returned investment is now about the amount needed for a **down payment** on the Valencia home, while in 1975 you could've purchased *two of them* for cash! Today you'd have two properties worth $1.5 million, both producing rental income.

An equally compelling example is the traditional method of buying property with a 10% down payment. The bond investor could've purchased *20 properties* worth $970,000 in 1975 with the same $100,000.00. For the past 30 years the property would have been rented and the mortgage paid off by the tenants. Today, those 20 properties would be worth some $15 million, and you'd be earning income from those 20 homes of about *$40,000 per month*.

Considering the fact that most real estate investors reinvest their equity in more property over time, the collective estate could now be worth more than $100 million. Of course, the other scenario is that you'd simply get your $100,000 back and buy more bonds. Do you have any lingering doubts why I refer to bonds as a depreciable asset? Case closed!

By the way, if you want to know my formula for growing your investment portfolio, just refer to my "FiveYear Plan," which involves refinancing as soon as your property has grown in value by 50% and then you buy two more homes from the proceeds. I'll be sharing more about that, naturally. Please read on!

Chapter 3

Taking Charge Of Your Life

If you're like most people, you don't see yourself working for the rest of your life. If you're smart, you're aware that if you don't provide for your own retirement, no one else will. Social Security was never meant to be the sole or even primary retirement option for Americans, and the system is so hopelessly broken so you can't count on it to allow a dignified retirement. Very few companies still offer pensions, and those that do offer them may not even be around, or solvent, by the time you retire. So you can't count on the government or your boss to pay for your retirement.

Just putting your money in the bank won't get it done, either. You'll lose the value of your money to inflation a lot more quickly than you'll ever grow it into a sizable retirement account. So a traditional savings account isn't the answer. You know all this. So you've tried investing in securities and perhaps commodities, in order to multiply your retirement dollars. You might even have opened a 401(k), expecting great results. But instead of making money, if you're like many people, you're either treading water, or actually going backwards. By the way, for the record, a 401K was introduced to employers as a great employee retention program initially. Not a retirement program. And it has worked well to keep employees from leaving and forfeiting those "Matching Funds" from their employer. And you thought it was a retirement program ?

Don't feel bad. You're not alone.

Individual investors invariably come to the conclusion that the securities market exists not to enrich ordinary people but instead to make the fat cats on Wall Street even fatter. Yes, there are ordinary people who have made sizable money in investments, but there are a lot more people who have lost their shirts. I want to share with you some evidence about the failure of securities and commodities as meaningful investments for regular investors like you and me. Pretty much the only way to make money in the stock or commodities markets is to become a broker or a dealer. Investing as a "little guy" in stocks, bonds, or commodities is highly unlikely to help you achieve your goal of a financially secure retirement. Let's see why.

The Stock Market

When people talk about "the stock market," they're usually referring to the S&P 500 Index, a collection of stocks the value of which is the benchmark that the financial industry uses in order to measure itself. If an investment "beat the market," that generally means that it did better than the S&P 500 Index for the comparable period of time. Over time, the stock market indeed does go up. But by how much? And how steadily does it make its progress? And does it go up enough to make sense as an investment to pay for your retirement?

Not by a long shot.

If your stock market investments did as well as the benchmark S&P 500 Index, you would have made only 7.9 percent a year on your money, going all the way back to 1960. Of course, this is before commissions, fees, and taxes, so your actual rate of return—the money that finally winds up in your pocket—is even smaller. And the key words here are "on average." There's no guarantee that your stock choices will perform as well as the S&P 500 Index. And there's no guarantee that you'll come into the market at a time when it's going up. There are years and sometimes multi-year periods where the market goes down and everybody loses money—except for the people charging those commissions and fees. They do well no matter how badly the market does.

Let's look at the record. If your investments match the performance of the S&P 500, you will realize consistent gains of around 10.4% per year. This results in a compound annual growth rate (CAGR) of 383% since 1960, 237% since 1980, and 66% since 1995. That sounds like a lot...until you realize that the average annual return of the S&P 500 since 1960 is the modest 7.9% I mentioned a moment ago.

If you put $1,000 into the stock market in 1960, and again, your success matched the S&P 500, you would have had slightly more than $23,000 at the end of 2005. A $5,000 investment would have grown to just above $115,000. With the stock market, though, timing is everything, and timing is mostly about luck, good or bad. If you entered the market between 1999 and 2001, you would have a loss by the beginning of 2006. If you entered before that time, you would have earned substantial returns. Luck is no substitute for the virtual certainty of growth that real estate provides.

Remember also that these figures do not reflect the costs associated with buying, selling and holding stocks. You can only determine your true returns—the money you can actually put in your pocket—when you subtract commission costs and capital gains taxes.

Exhibit 1

1960	1970	1980	1990	2000	2005
$1,000	$1,529	$2,053	$9,776	$25,083	$23,024
$5,000	$7,646	$10,266	$48,878	$125,415	$115,123
$10,000	$15,292	$20,523	$97,756	$250,830	$230,245

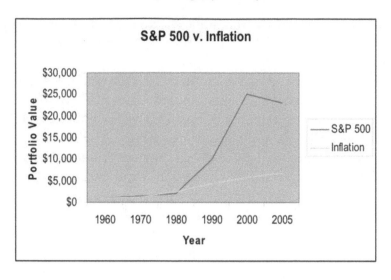

The New York Stock Exchange

The oldest securities exchange in the United States, the New York Stock Exchange (NYSE), has become synonymous with the equity securities industry itself. The NYSE is a traditional stock exchange. It's famous for harried dealers rushing around on its frenetic trading floor, which is covered with trails of paper despite the automated trading systems that the market employs. The NYSE trades shares of stock of the country's most valuable and prestigious companies. Like the Dow-Jones Industrial Average, the NYSE is a key indicator of the state of the American economy. The NYSE moves more slowly than other broad measures of the market, which limits the opportunity for big, quick gains.

If you had invested in a basket of NYSE stocks, your results would be determined by when you plunked your money down. CAGR since 1971 is a robust 269%, with a strong 233% CAGR since 1980. Since 2000, though, the NYSE has been stagnant, with a CAGR of only 2.68%. With the exception of dips after the dotcom collapse and 9/11, the NYSE has essentially offered slow and measured growth since 2000. The NYSE requires a long-term buy and hold investment strategy with few opportunities for short-term gains.

If you put $1,000 into the NYSE in 1966, you would have approximately $13,752 at the end of 2005. A $5,000 investment would have grown to almost $69,000. Those post-2000 dips would have resulted in declines for new entrants to the market, though the index had recovered from the beginning of 2005 and had approximately returned to its dotcom boom position by the beginning of 2006.

Exhibit 2

1966	1970	1980	1990	2000	2005
$1,000	$1,033	$1,242	$3,912	$13,042	$13,752
$5,000	$5,167	$6,212	$19,559	$65,212	$68,759
$ 10,000	$10,335	$12,425	$39,117	$130,424	$137,518

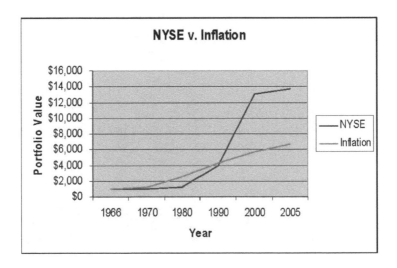

Adjusted for inflation, $1,000 invested in 1960 would require $6,701 at the beginning of 2006. While an investment in the NYSE would outpace inflation, with a real return of $7,050, representing a CAGR of 43%.

The NASDAQ

Maybe you think that high tech is the way to beat the market. It isn't. The dotcom bust of the early 2000s left millions of investors with huge losses. Unfortunately, these individuals and are even further from retirement than when they started investing. The NASDAQ, the stock exchange where many high tech companies' stocks are traded, has been coming back slowly. But unless you're absolutely certain that you've picked the next hot stock, investing in high tech won't get you where you want to go.

Over the past three decades, the NASDAQ has grown exponentially, to the point where this exchange has overtaken the American Stock Exchange as the second most widely used exchange for American investors. If you were wise, or fortunate, to buy into the NASDAQ in past decades, you would have done very well. The CAGR on a portfolio of all NASDAQ stocks: 360% since 1971, 206% since 1980, and 125% since 1990. Unfortunately, the longer you waited to buy NASDAQ, the smaller your returns. The burst of the dotcom bubble in 2000 and subsequent economic weakness means that if you bought the NASDAQ and held it until 2006, you would have lost thirteen percent a year on your money.

NASDAQ investments, like all stock investments, require a long-term buy and hold strategy. An investment of $1,000 in 1971 would be worth $16,560 in 2005, but it would have been worth $21,468 in 2000.

Exhibit 3

1971	1980	1990	2000	2005
$ 1,000	$1,773	$3,726	$21,468	$16,560
$ 5,000	$8,865	$16,379	$108,242	$82,800
$ 10,000	$17,730	$32,759	$216,484	$165,600

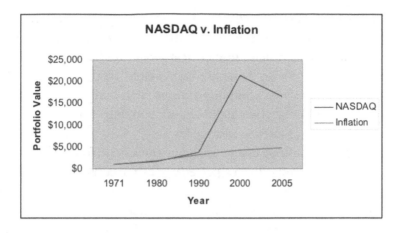

Adjusted for inflation, $1,000 invested in 1971 would require $4,870 at the beginning of 2006. An investment in the NASDAQ would outpace inflation with a real return of $11,690, representing a CAGR of 84%.

Stocks Versus Real Estate

The bottom line: If you want to grow your money in a meaningful, predictable way, the stock market isn't the place for you. Statistically, you're likely to outpace inflation. But you won't get the explosive growth you need in order to fund the retirement you desire.

Keep in mind that the people who want to sell you stocks will tell you repeatedly that over the long haul, stocks go up more in value than does real estate. I was in the brokerage industry for twenty-two years, and I'm not surprised at all to see stock peddlers telling you this same thing over and over again. Don't believe them, because they're comparing apples to oranges, and I'll show you why that's the case.

It's actually very simple. When you buy stock, you have to pay one hundred percent of the cost of the stock. When you buy real estate, however, you only have to pay ten or twenty percent of the cost as a down payment. As long as you service your mortgage and take care of your tenants, if you have any, you're all set. So when you're comparing the return on investment for stocks versus real estate, you're comparing investments you made with 100% of the purchase price versus investments you made with only ten to twenty percent. Leverage favors real estate and makes a Hugh difference.

This means that over a ten or twenty or thirty year period, the stock market as a whole may move up at a higher percentage rate than real estate, you still make much more on real estate. Radically more. That's because you were able to purchase real estate literally with dimes on the dollar, whereas when you bought stock, you had to pay a hundred percent of the cost of the stock. Unless you buy on margin which increases your risk of loosing money faster.

You might be thinking that you can buy stock on margin, which means that you are only putting down a percentage of the cost of the stock at the time you purchase it. Buying stock on margin is one of the riskiest moves an investor can make. That's because if the value of the stock dips below the 50% margin requirements, your broker will make a dreaded "margin call" to you, and that means that you've got to write a check, there and then, to cover the difference necessary to maintain the 50% maintenance level. You take 100% of the risk on margin. If the stock drops further, you can count on another margin call and another one after that. A dip in the stock market or a dip in a particular stock you've purchased on margin can have disastrous consequences for your financial health and you can loose 100% of your money if you don't act quickly. Please take a look at our YouTube video http://www.youtube.com/watch?v=cvm8u8JhFzY titled "Are You Smarter Than a Stockbroker".

By contrast, if a piece of real estate you own drops in value for a period of time, it doesn't matter … as long as you are able to keep up your mortgage payments. And if you've got a tenant or the money to keep up those mortgage payments, you don't have to worry about a thing. Don't let anybody tell you that investing in the stock market beats investing in real estate. Okay, maybe you'll be the lucky one who catches a Google or a Yahoo type of stock at the right moment. But let's face it—that's not smart investing. That's just dumb luck. And we can't count on luck, smart or dumb, to get us to our financial goals.

What About Commodities?

Okay, if stocks aren't the answer, what about commodities? Can't you make a small fortune investing in valuable commodities like gold or oil?

The only way you can make a small fortune in these commodities… is to start with a large fortune.

Let's start with gold, whose value is clear to everyone. It's the ultimate conservative investment, the thing investors and governments have turned to during depressions, wars, terrorist acts, and anything else that triggers fear. There's only one problem with gold. It's a lousy investment if you're thinking about retirement. As I write these words, gold is over $600 an ounce and has risen since the terrorist attacks on September 11, 2001. But let's say you had bought gold at any point in the past twenty-five years. Chances are that you would have been waiting years or even decades for gold to increase in value. And if peace somehow breaks out in the world, the value of gold is likely to start falling again. It practically always has. In short, don't believe the hype about gold or any other precious metal. Investing in gold won't bring you any closer to your retirement day, and may well end up postponing it. Also, you buy gold for cash and it doesn't pay and dividends. You might have to pay storage fees also.

Now let's examine the gold's recent history more closely. Since 1961, gold has grown at a CAGR of 280%. After a weak decade in the 1960s, gold gained momentum, spiking in the late 1970s. The unusually rapid growth of gold through the early 1980s was followed by a precipitous decline, from which it has only started to recover in the wake of the 9/11 terror attacks. If you invested in gold in 1960 you would have yielded a solid return. If you bought in 1981, when gold peaked above $600 an ounce, you'd still be looking to break even, twenty five years later. And during that time, you would not have received interest or any other return despite having tied up your money for 25 years. Doesn't sound like too good a bet, does it? And you cannot leverage your invest but if you could you would loose your money even quicker.

If you invested $1,000 in gold in 1960, you would have approximately $14,431 at the end of 2006 . A $5,000 investment would have grown to just above $70,000. Any investment after the gold crash of the early 1980s would show consistent growth, but investors who got in before 1980 and have held their gold positions still are waiting to break even.

The bottom line: gold is for wearing, not for investing. The people who make money in commodities are the brokers, not the investors!

Exhibit 4

1960	1970	1980	1990	2000	2005
$1,00000	$1,066	$16,299	$10,581	$7,470	$4,055
$5,0000	$5,329	$81,493	$52,904	$37,349	$70,274
$10,000	$10,658	$162,986	$105,808	$74,699	$140,548

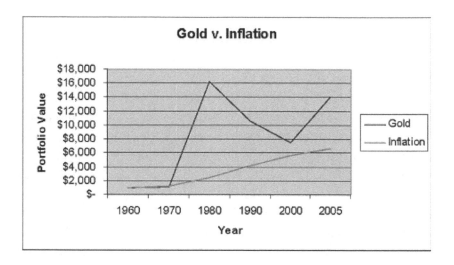

Adjusted for inflation, $1,000 invested in 1960 would require $6,701 at the beginning of 2006. An investment in gold would outpace inflation, with a real return of $8,043 and an actual CAGR of 184% over 25 years. Of course in 1960 you could buy a house for $15,000 that rose in value to over $500,000 by 2005. With normal real estate leverage, such an investment would have exceeded a 5,000% ROI. Now *that's* a bling-bling!

Oil

Oil made a millionaire out of ol' Jed Clampett...so why not you, too?

Wouldn't it be smart to trade oil futures, since the price of gas seems to be going up and up and up?

In a word, no. Investing in oil is almost a certain way to lose money, or, at best, break even. Everybody thinks that the price of oil has been shooting up over the last few years, but if you look at the numbers, the actual price of oil has risen at a rate *slower than inflation* for the last two decades. If you invested a thousand dollars in oil in 1986, and if you were still holding it twenty years later, you'd be barely breaking even, relative to inflation. Oil and gas will fuel your car, but not your retirement.

Exhibit 5

1986	1990	2000	2005
$1,000	$1,381	$1,047	$1,609
$5,000	$6,905	$5,235	$8,403
$10,000	$13,810	$10,470	$16,085

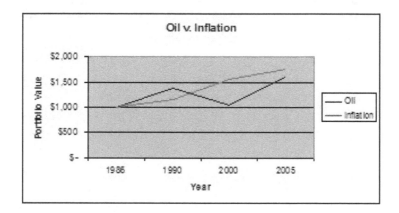

Adjusted for inflation, $1,000 invested in 1986 would require $1,757 at the beginning of 2006. The real return on an investment in oil, relative to inflation, is $148 which yields a negative CAGR of 8.5%

Are We Rich Yet?

If you are invested in the stock market or in commodities, there are two ways to find out whether you are making money or not on any given day. One approach is to subscribe to all the financial newspapers, magazines, and websites that give you up-to-the-minute information on your investments. The simpler way is to simply tape an index card with the word NO in capital letters to your refrigerator. Every time you pass the refrigerator and glance at that sign, you'll know whether you're making money on your securities and commodities investments. It's a lot cheaper and it's a lot less time-consuming to put up that index card than to track the stock market and the commodities market. Better still, you can save all that money that you've been spending on subscriptions.

But Chuck, I've Got a 401(k)!

I'm glad you do. But if you're counting on your 401(k) plan to fund your retirement, that may be a riskier bet than you might ever have imagined. As an article in the February, 2006 issue of Benefits & Compensation Digest points out, the whole 401(k) plan system is an "experiment" less than two decades old. We don't even know if it's an experiment that's really going to work! But overwhelming evidence already makes clear that relying on your 401(k) to fund your retirement is a recipe for disaster. Here are some of the reasons why:

- It's not a stable, long-term approach to savings. There's no rule that says you have to put money aside, so many people don't.
- Few people are taking full advantage of their 401(k)—only ten percent of those with 401(k)s fully fund it. To fully fund a 401(k) requires an ongoing level of discipline that most of us, sad to say, don't have.
- You can take cash out of a 401(k), and many people do so, well in advance of their retirement. This means that their money never has a chance to grow. That piggy bank full of cash is just too tempting for mere mortals like ourselves.
- Most people in this country are not investment experts ... so they're making poor or uninformed choices about what funds to own in their 401(k) plans.
- Most 401(k) plans simply offer a menu of mutual funds, and most mutual funds, as you'll see in detail in a future Chapter, fail to keep up with either inflation or the stock market as a whole.
- There are relatively high expenses attached to maintaining a

401(k) plan, and those expenses get passed on to the individual investors.

- One-quarter of employees entitled to open 401(k) plans don't even bother doing so.

The result, according to Benefits & Compensation Digest: "a wide spectrum of winners and losers." Most of that spectrum is where you don't want to end up.

A 401(k) plan, in short, is not a ticket to a guaranteed, stable retirement. If anything, it's a ticket to never retiring at all.

For you and me, the two best ways to make real money are to start your own business (a risky proposition, since most new businesses fail), or invest in real estate. Real estate contains risks,

Of course, but I'm here to show you how to eliminate the risk by faithfully following the successful formula I'm offering you in this book.

People with a 401K are always asking whether they should continue to make contributions when their rate of growth is usually very small if at all. Many 401K programs actually loose money over time but fortunately there are some that don't. I like to give people an honest answer based upon my many years experience handling pension money for my clients. To give an honest answer, I have to ask questions in order to know how their 401K money is performing. I try to determine the average rate of return but that can be hard without knowing how much was contributed and when. Usually, I use the best available information which is the latest end of the year statement. Rarely do I find a retirement fund worth contributing to and that includes 401K's et. al.

The client usually explains the most compelling reason for continuing is the employer contribution which sometimes equals their own. For example the employee puts in $1,000. and the employer matches it. Good so far but that matching contribution comes with a price. You may not get it at all if you leave the company too soon. Or, you may not borrow against it or take a withdrawal for a designated period of time. There's a variety of reasons why the matching contribution may not have a big impact on your retirement account because of the restrictions.

So, let's compare your 401K with 100% matching funds from

your employer to a simple Investment Real Estate purchase with 10% down and 90% financing. In the real estate purchase you get matching funds amounting to 900% of your contribution which is better than your employers 100% matching contribution. As an example, you buy a piece of income property for $100,000 and put a $10,000 down payment. The balance of the purchase price comes from a lender who puts the other $90,000. That's 900% better than your 401K and you get 100% of the benefits of owning the property immediately as well as immediate tax benefits which exceed the tax benefits generated from a 401K.. The only condition is that you must repay the 90% loan. But you get 100% of the tax write off, 100% of the appreciation, 100% of the rent less expenses and 100% of the depreciation. You can sell when you want or keep the property forever and let the tenants pay off your loan. So, I ask you, given the choice of getting matching funds on your 401K with the restrictions that go with it vs. putting 10% down and getting 100% of the benefits with only one restriction (you must repay the loan) which is the better choice?

But what about the tax write-off you ask? You can deduct the contribution to your 401K but you can only deduct the amount of your contribution. In real estate, you get 100% of the benefits and 100% of the depreciation even though you only invested 10% of the purchase price. So you are actually receiving more tax benefits if you make NO contribution to a retirement account and invest your retirement money in investment real estate instead. If you invest in a growth area of the country, you will actually out perform the best performing retirement accounts by more than 10 to 1. When we go through the numbers and stick to the facts (and forget about the minor tax benefits available for a modest retirement account contribution) most people decide for themselves that further contributions to a retirement account is the worst choice they can make. The system is truly broken and no amount of contribution will fix it. Buying and owning real estate is the best way to prepare for retirement.

The conclusion about your 401K is the same if you have an IRA, Keogh, Sep IRA or Roth IRA. Despite the remote possibility that you might make money in your Roth and be able to defer those gains, I can't imagine anyone thinking that a Roth IRA is worth considering for even a moment of your time. The retirement system in the US is broken and offers false assurances that somehow they will perform better in the future than they've done in the past. For most Americans, the realization that their retirement account system will not provide retirement security is realized when they retire but then it's too late.

That leaves Social Security but everyone knows by now that that is nothing more than grocery money. So, what do you invest in to improve your yield and provide growth and financial security when you retire. Investment Real Estate is the number one way and done properly with the assistance of experienced professionals will out perform any investments offered by Securities Firms, Commodities Firms, Banks and Insurance Companies. Since 85% of the wealth of this country is represented by Real Estate holdings and the tax benefits are greater than any retirement account, the decision to retire with dignity is a personal one. However, the facts are in and real estate is the best way to invest for retirement. For further guidelines go to www. TenPercentDown.com and register.

Why does Wall Street make so much money for itself? Because it has so many paying customers. When you own real estate, you're the one with the paying customers—they're called tenants. Read this book over and over again until you completely grasp this system for buying and owning real estate, and you'll be able to retire with dignity when you want to. You'll also be able to teach these same investing skills to your children and grandchildren, so they don't get ripped off and so that they can build their own wealth. If you're sick and tired of being taken advantage of by the investment industry, and you're ready to roll up your sleeves and make some real money, then keep reading.

Chapter 4

Mutual Funds Make Money –
But Not For You

If you have money invested in a mutual fund, you're not alone. At this writing, 48% of American households own mutual funds and are relying on those funds to help fund their retirement. There's only one problem. The great American love affair with mutual funds is entirely one-sided. We love them, but they don't love us back. In this chapter, I want to show you why mutual funds are actually a rip-off for the average investor and a billion dollar moneymaker for Wall Street. If you still want to own your mutual funds by the time you have read to the end of this chapter, then I haven't done my job.

Let's start with a definition of what mutual funds are all about. In theory, a mutual fund is a collection of stocks selected by a seasoned investment professional for the benefit of the many contributors to that fund. This professional studies the market and buys and sells stocks in order to make you money. When mutual funds first came into existence, they were the cheapest, simplest, and often the safest way for individuals to buy stock. Today, of course, you can go online and get access to a vast amount of information about stocks, and you can make your own decisions. And then you can trade them yourself for as little as $8 a transaction when you go online. Do I recommend that? No, but this option didn't exist back when mutual funds began. So maybe they were a good deal fifty years ago. But not anymore.[7]

There's not a single reason to go into mutual funds today, and as you're about to discover, there are billions of reasons for you to stay away from them. Mutual funds, to put it simply, are dangerous to your financial health. And if you think you're going to be able to retire on a mutual fund, think again.

Mutual fund managers are paid a half-million to a million dollars a year or more, but they aren't judged on how much money they make for you. Instead, they are judged—and given raises and bonuses—on how much new money they can attract to the fund.

You might think that if they do a great job for you, they would automatically attract more money to the fund. The reality is that your interests and the interests of the fund manager are worlds apart. Let's see how this works.

Consider fees. Most people think that mutual funds are a "cheap" investment, because you don't get a separate bill for trading in and out of the fund. In fact, Wall Street is too smart to let you know how much they're charging you for the privilege of, well, treading water financially. The mutual fund companies actually earn *a hundred billion dollars a year* on fees, almost all of which are partially or completely hidden to the investing public. There are fees when you invest. There are fees when you sell. And there are fees when you simply hold the fund, which they use for advertising, telemarketing, and other expenses. In other words, the mutual fund is spending *your* hard-earned investment money…to attract other investors!

Where do those fees come from? They certainly don't come out of the salary of the fund manager, or the bonuses he or she will receive for attracting even more money from people like you. If you own mutual funds, you are part of an annual hundred-billion-dollar wealth transfer from the American people to the companies that manage the funds.

Some investors recognize the fact that mutual funds are divided between "load" funds and "no-load." A load fund explicitly charges upfront fees, or loads, which are essentially commissions for the people who sold you the funds and their employer. Many investors choose to put their money into no-load funds, because they want to avoid those fees. I've got bad news for people who put their faith in no-load funds. No-load funds also carry huge—even whopping—fees.

How much? How about up to 1% of all the assets that the fund contains, each and every year? That's right— you *think* you're paying no fees at all. But instead, the fund is quietly deducting 1% or more of your entire holdings, year after year, and sticking them in their pocket.

We all know that technology has radically transformed the way investing takes place. But fund fees haven't decreased, despite that fact that it's cheaper and easier than ever to run a mutual fund. The mutual fund owners could have passed these savings onto you. But why should they? Their attitude: what you don't know won't hurt you.

You may be thinking, "It's okay to pay fees, because I've got the top investment professionals on Wall Street working for me." But how good a job are these top investment professionals really doing? The sad reality is that almost 80% of mutual funds under-perform benchmarks like the Standard and Poor's 500 or the Dow Jones Industrial Average. It sounds hard to believe, but it's true: four out of five mutual funds actually don't even keep pace with the market. Your fees are buying you an 80% likelihood that you'll do worse than the market as a whole.

The only place where mutual funds sound like outstanding investments is in the advertisements you see in financial magazines. But don't believe those ads for a minute. Mutual fund companies have countless ways to make their performance look much better than it really is. First, only the best funds in a fund family will ever make it into an advertisement. For every half-decent fund that a company offers, there might be half-a-dozen dogs that never get advertised. You won't be reading about them in an ad in *Forbes* or *Fortune*, because their returns are so poor. So don't think that if a company has one good fund, the other twenty it offers are just as good. If the other twenty were any good, they'd be in the advertisements, too! On top of that, there's something called "survivorship bias." That's a fancy way of saying that bad funds are killed off, and the mutual fund companies only report to their investors—or their potential customers—the "good news" about the mutual funds that somehow managed to survive. How many mutual funds actually disappear? Well, in the period from 1962 to 1993, one-third of all mutual funds disappeared. And it's not because they were making their investors a lot of money. They vanished because they did such a bad job. If you think that's bad, consider the 1990s as a whole. During that period, half of the mutual funds offered for sale disappeared from the marketplace. And again, all of these funds were managed by extremely high-paid—and theoretically highly-talented—money managers.

So what went wrong?

There are a lot of reasons why mutual funds fail to keep up with the stock market as a whole, let alone actually make money for their investors. Let's take a look at some of those reasons.

First, fund managers are often under a mandate from their bosses to be "fully invested." This means that they have an obligation to have a 100% of the money they manage actually invested in stocks at any given time. Let's say that a given fund manager likes 20 different stocks. Great—they're all in the portfolio. But that might only consume about 40% of the money he has to invest. Since he's got to be "fully invested," he'll go out and buy stocks he doesn't even like, just so he can fill out the rest of the portfolio. Otherwise, he'll be in trouble with his bosses? And with whom would he rather be in trouble, you or the people who pay his salary and bonuses.

Second, many mutual fund managers engage in a dubious practice called "pumping." This happens when the end of the quarter is approaching. Keep in mind that mutual funds are all judged on their performance each quarter. You care about how the fund does over the 30 years until your retirement. But the manager has to produce great numbers every single quarter…or they won't attract any more money into the fund, and that will be the end of their seven-figure salary and bonus.

Many mutual fund managers will actually buy up a lot of stock, simply to pump up the price of that stock for the few days right around the closing of the quarter. Once the quarter ends, those shares will almost certainly sink back to their actual lower value. The mutual fund manager is happy, because the value of the fund looks good at the end of the quarter. Buying and selling stock this way has nothing to do with taking care of your retirement. It's all about helping the fund manager put up good numbers.

But guess who paid for all those stock transactions, all that buying and the selling? That's right—you. And on top of that, if the stock actually went up during the brief period that the fund held it, you'll be paying short term capital gains tax...*even though you didn't pull any money out of the fund.* You're paying transaction fees—and taxes—on transactions that run counter to your desire to see the fund grow over a period of years. So pumping is another reason why mutual fund managers are not your friends.

Third, there's the question of capital gains taxes. I'll tell you who really loves mutual funds. It's Uncle Sam. The IRS makes billions of dollars every year from people like you, who are hit with short-term capital gains taxes whenever your mutual fund manager sells stock. Have you ever opened up your year-end report for the mutual fund, only to find out that you owe capital gains tax? You're probably sitting there scratching your head saying, "How can I owe any tax? I never sold any stock!" That's right, you didn't sell stock, but the manager of your fund did, on your behalf. You are considered an owner of that stock, so you are liable for the tax. In fact, your fund could go down over the course of the year...and you could still owe both short term and long term capital gains taxes. Remember that the IRS is not coming after the mutual fund company or the manager of the fund for that tax money. They're coming after *you.*

Fourth, your mutual fund manager might be "twotiming" you. Every year, more and more mutual fund managers are also managing hedge funds for investment companies. A hedge fund is a high risk/ potentially high return investment, usually open only to the wealthiest investors. This can create a clear conflict of interest for the manager who is in charge of "your" mutual fund and some super rich person's hedge fund investment. I'll show you how it works. Let's say that the fund manager has great success with a particular stock. Where is he going to put the winnings from that investment? In the mutual fund...or in the hedge fund? Don't be naïve enough to think that mutual fund investors will get a "taste" of those winnings. As Donnie Brasco says, "Fuggetaboutit."

Most holders of mutual funds are not sophisticated enough to notice whether their fund managers are sticking their biggest "wins" in the hedge fund pot. Hedge fund investors, by and large, are more sophisticated than mutual fund investors. They know what's going on, and they will be far more aware of—and appreciative of—a big win than mutual fund investors. So you definitely run the risk of being two-timed.

You might ask, "How could my mutual fund company commit such a blatant conflict of interest?" They'll defend themselves by telling you, the media, the Securities and Exchange Commission, or anybody else who has the intelligence to ask, that it's really no big deal. If they don't let their mutual fund managers run hedge funds as well, then those great managers will quit the company and go run hedge funds for somebody else. So they have to allow this conflict of interest to exist simply to protect themselves.

Of course, since four out of five mutual funds under-perform the market, you'd be better off if your mutual fund manager left and if they just stuck your money in a fund that tracks the Standard and Poor's 500! Of course, you'd be even better off if you've never invested in a mutual fund in the first place, but they'll never tell *you* that.

Fifth, remember what I said a moment ago—mutual fund managers are paid not to make you money, but to attract more money into their mutual fund. You know and I know that the bigger the risk, the bigger the profit. That's just as true for the mutual fund manager as it is for anyone else. So mutual fund managers think nothing of risking large sums of money to create large returns…to attract new money into the fund and to make themselves look great in the process.

There's only one problem here. Who's money are they putting at risk? That's right, yours. So what's the downside of considerable risk? That's right. Losing everything. But it's not going to be the manager who loses everything. It's just you.

Sixth, mutual funds are commonly marketed with the idea that if a fund did well in the past, it's going to do well in the future. That's why a fund that has a really great return in one quarter or one year, or one five-year period, will receive prominent play in advertising. Again, the whole idea is to attract more money into the fund, and nothing succeeds like success. Unfortunately, it's just as tough to repeat success with a mutual fund as it is in any other competitive endeavor. How many baseball teams have won the World Series twice in a row lately? How many football teams have won the Super Bowl more than once a decade? And how many mutual funds actually sustained their top dog position for very long? Precious few. A lot fewer than the mutual fund industry will have you believe.

I hope by now you agree that mutual funds are not all they're cracked up to be. If you want to spend $1,400 a year or more in fees for every $100,000 you have invested, then you probably still like the idea of mutual funds.[19] If you don't mind losing your share of billions of dollars to the mutual fund and brokerage industries, and if you don't mind paying short term and long term capital gains tax on stocks from which you never profited, then maybe you'd like to keep investing in mutual funds.

And if you do, maybe you'd like to buy a bridge as well!

P. T. Barnum had it right when he called Americans a nation of suckers. We want to believe that financial institutions have our best interest at heart. They spend billions of dollars every year promoting that concept in their advertising. Don't believe it for a minute. The only bottom line they're thinking about is their own, not yours. Yes, Americans love mutual funds. But the feeling…isn't mutual.

Chapter 5

Basics Of Real Estate Investing

What Do You Buy and How Do You Buy It?

Now we get to the part that justifies the cost of this book many times over. I've invested in property for more than 40 years, attended many seminars, and purchased many books and tapes. I've tried buying property using almost every "sure fire" method promoted for the past three decades. I'll mention a few of them. Still, quite frankly, I just don't want to waste your time with explanations of why most of these purchase plans consistently fail to get the same results we're getting now.

For starters, I'm convinced that it's not worth the additional time required to find and buy properties that are distressed, fixer-uppers or foreclosures. Let's accept the principle that you get what you pay for. Many people have come to me after my seminars and told me about "what a great buy" they got—typically, a bargain-priced property offered by sellers desperate to avoid foreclosure. I don't deny that you might get lucky occasionally, but not without a great deal of time and effort. Bargains don't fall into your lap; you have to look for them. Other would-be investors are searching too.

Those who are focused on profiting from other people's misfortunes are called "bottom feeders." They're in the same category as "ambulance chasers." I'm not one of them because (a) I don't have the time to pursue this strategy and (b) I'm looking for a different type of property.

During my 22 years as a stockbroker and investment banker with some of Wall Street's finest firms, I enjoyed a high income. My accountant suggested that I needed more tax write-offs and encouraged me to buy real estate. I did just that over a period of about five years. I knew little about real estate—except what I'd learned buying a new home occasionally as I moved up the social ladder. I made money because I worked hard and "sold" a lot of investment products to my clients. I truly believed that a person could get rich if he or she bought the products offered by my firm. It took me many years to discover that the people who became my clients were already wealthy.

At my investment seminars, I tell the story of a millionaire who made a generous contribution to a local charity. He was asked by a local reporter how he became a millionaire. He replied, "I owe it all to my stockbroker." The reporter asked the donor what he was before he met his broker, and the donor replied," A multi-millionaire." Then there was the stockbroker who won a million dollars in the lottery. Asked what he was going to do with his winnings, and he replied, "I think I'll just keep investing them until it's all gone."

To build my Stock Brokerage/ Consultant business, I hosted a weekly radio show on KMNY and was an occasional guest on T.V. shows offering financial information. I was always a member of the Chairman's Council (Top 5% producer) and was certainly looked upon as a professional and had the large office and supporting staff to encourage my desire to be the largest producer in the office. I got to the point that my potential clients had to prove that they had a million dollar portfolio before my secretary made an appointment for them to visit me. I was busy with many activities including being a member of the Board of Directors of Sensotron (a small public company), Deacon and Board member of the Crystal Cathedral and a Board Member of Martin Luther Hospital.

Being the largest producer doesn't mean that my clients make more money and enjoyed better results than the other Brokers/ Financial Advisors, et al. Being a Top Producer just means that I "sold" more products, earned more commissions and made more money for "The Firm." I didn't want to loose money for my clients but many of the products did not perform as well as the Firm or Wholesaler promised. Yes, they assured us that the projections were reasonable and sometimes even conservative but we couldn't make the same promises to the clients. After all, if we fail then the client can hold us (The Broker) responsible by filing an arbitration (Complaint). "After all" Mr. Salisbury, "didn't you know that a Real Estate Partnership sponsored by Prudential Securities for the benefit of Holiday Inns so that they can expand and build numerous Hampton Inns at prime locations might fail?" Actually, I never gave it a second thought because the Company promoted it as having huge growth potential that would provide income and growth. After all, Prudential was as "Solid as The Rock" weren't they? Why would they lie to me? The partnership didn't fail but failed to make any of the original projections and was not the safe, secure investment promised by Prudential.

While I was still one of those stockbrokers, selling "secure" investments to my clients, I ventured out to acquire some real estate on my own. I contacted a local Realtor® who, by all accounts, earned only a fraction of my income. But I suspected he know more about locating income property than I did. So I told him I needed some income property to reduce to my tax obligation. I soon purchased several fourplexes that had some deferred maintenance for a very good price.

I also picked up a duplex in a prime location that looked good on the outside but had some potential termite issues on the inside. The agent didn't tell me about the termite issue and suggested that I grab the property quickly and forgo a termite inspection. I got my tax write-offs and then some! The tenants in the fourplex were not the kind of renters I would have picked, and the property needed a lot of work to attract higher-quality tenants. I began the fix-up, but the maintenance issues kept growing.

The duplex was a hassle as well, mainly because of a serious termite infestation. I thought, if this is what it takes to gain a tax advantage, then I'm quickly losing interest. Sure, I got my tax write-off—and major headaches too! I only put 10% down but I was putting more money in every month which just increased the amount of my investment. Before my first anniversary I called the agent that sold me the property and told him to liquidate as soon as possible. Of course, I told him to find a buyer for the duplex that wouldn't require a termite inspection. Today, termite inspections are required but in the early 1980's it wasn't required…it was optional.

As a part of my real estate education, I decided to buy land and build "new" apartments. After all, new property would require little maintenance, and I'd attract better tenants, get a higher rent and avoid the headaches. Because land in California was expensive, I began looking in Arizona. I had a brother living in Phoenix and other relatives in Glendale, so I contacted another well-educated real estate agent and asked him to help me find land in a developed area that was large enough for me to build at least 24 apartments.

I also acquired some nice lots suitable for new fourplexes as well as eight nearly completed units that were owned by a savings and loan. I agreed to buy them if the S&L completed those units so they'd be ready to rent. The S&L kept its part of the agreement, and I added the units to my growing portfolio. I hired a talented architect to design the fourplexes and asked several builders to bid on the project. Before long I owned two new fourplexes across the street from the four duplexes that I purchased from the S&L.

The architect then started work on planning the new apartment complex and was able to locate 36 units, a structure for four washers and two dryers, and a pool on the L-shaped property. A year later I had another 36 units to add to the 16 that I already owned. I was realizing some great tax benefits and actually bought additional land within a block of my new complex.

Although I wasn't involved in renting the units, I quickly learned that I had a high vacancy rate and felt increasing pressure to attract more tenants. I found new property managers and offered bonuses to agencies in Phoenix to help find additional renters. To complicate the scenario even further, nonpayment of rent and other circumstances forced me to evict some tenants—a touchy and time-consuming process. More and more I saw that the multiplying headaches, which were time consuming and costly, far outweighed any tax benefits.

Although I wanted people with good credit I would have to get used to the higher vacancies if I wasn't flexible with that rule. Seems like some people would loose their job and not pay rent so we had to start eviction. That would make them mad so they would take it out on my brand new apartments. Pride of ownership...I seemed to be the only one who had it. In my process of education I learned that property in Glendale, Arizona was cheap and rents were low because there was an overabundance of low income families and modern day cowboys who rode motorcycles instead of horses. I was working like a "horse" to keep up the payments on my properties, paid for the repairs and the evictions just so I could "enjoy" the tax benefits. What tax benefits... these were real losses? I was loosing a bunch of money. My future was on hold and it wasn't fun anymore. My rental income mogul image was being damaged by losers. They wondered why I was so concerned about them paying their rent on time. After all, I was rich...I could afford to give them a break. I was compassionate and I did give many breaks and I discovered that people soon expect it.

I was consulting with business owners and would never have allowed them to run their business the way I was running my income real estate business. I originally looked at it as a tax benefit but it turned out to be a business and it was loosing money. I was dealing with people that I had no interest in dealing with and my patience was severely limited. I soon started listing the properties and eventually sold everything. My loss was someone else's headache. Now I was sour on real estate as an investment. After all, I was in the investment and consulting business. I was a professional. What was I doing providing housing for these losers?

It was years later that I finally learned to profit from my mistakes. I could have and should have purchased property in Scottsdale, Ariz., or even Orange County, Calif., where I lived. Yes, I would have paid more for the land. Even so, had I built the same quality units in a *better location* and attracted *higher-quality tenants*, I might still own those properties today. In hindsight, I wish I'd done exactly that!

You don't get good tenants when you're renting in bad neighborhoods. Whether you're a buyer or a builder, you need to attract responsible tenants who will care for your properties as if they were their own and, for the next 30 years, pay off your mortgage while you enjoy the appreciation and the tax benefits.

So what did I learn after three decades of buying, building, selling and renting various parcels of real estate? I learned a specific set of rules that I believe represent the safest and most conservative way to own property, enjoy the tax benefits and earn substantial growth for one's investment capital.

To ensure that you're able to handle your mortgage payments with no delays and no sleepless nights, the first rule is: **Find the best tenants**. They're easy to identify. They have a 680 or better credit score, pay their rent on time and have no criminal record. You must verify all three to be sure that you have suitable "partners" to retire the mortgage on your property.

Getting the credit score is easy; so is completing the background check. As for timely payment of rent, you'll need to contact the prospect's prior landlord and ask him or her directly about that matter. Usually, the landlord will tell you the truth. The exception is when a landlord is eager to get rid of a tenant and hopes that you'll accept that person. Under those circumstances, you have to use your keen instincts.

In order to attract the best tenants, it's essential to observe this second major rule as well: **Always buy *new* properties from reputable builders in desirable locations**. Given the choice of renting a new home or a used residence, tenants will pick the new home every time. What's more, the builder will always warranty the home in case tenants encounter some initial maintenance problems. Bear in mind that if you don't like the floor plan or the location, prospective tenants probably won't either. And you can't change the location or the floor plan. Once you buy it you own it and the debt that goes with it. That may be forever.

I say "forever" because I do *not* recommend selling good property. Refinance it or get a line of credit against the equity, but don't sell. I strongly suggest that you buy property, hold it and build an estate that will take care of you, your children and grandchildren. You'll depreciate it over 27½ years and pay it off in 30 years. The equity you build will help you purchase many more properties over the years.

To get comfortable with the idea of buying and holding, just ask yourself this question: How would I like to still own every piece of real estate that I've ever owned? Obviously, the intensity of your answer depends upon how much property you've owned.

I remember the first home I purchased. It was in Bloomington, Ill., and the price was about $12,000. It was a large two-story residence with an apartment upstairs. The next one was a beautiful new one-story home in Springfield, Ill., that I bought for $20,000 with a monthly payment of $200. The third house, which I bought in 1975 for $48,500, was in Valencia, Calif. (four bedrooms, 3½ baths with about 2,000 sq. ft.). Today the value of those three homes is about $1.4 million, and they'd be paid off by now. I'd currently be generating a minimum of $3,400 a month of rental income. If I add my subsequent three homes to the list, the value of my portfolio would be $6.5 million and monthly rental income would range from $15,000 to $18,000. Yes, buying and holding is a *solid* plan. That's how you build an estate!

The third major rule is just as important as the first two when it comes to producing maximum return on your investment. It's actually a two-fold principle: **(1) Never pay more than 10 to 20% down on any property**; and **(2) Take steps to avoid a large negative cash flow when you close escrow and rent the property**. If you can buy with less than 10% down, you should do so. Obviously, with good credit you'll have better opportunities for favorable financing.

It's important to note that builders always prefer that you use their chosen lenders. They frequently offer incentives for you to do so. But those incentives come at a price. Using the builder's lender could mean you'll pay a higher interest rate and experience a negative cash flow.

To secure optimum financing, deal with lenders that offer a short-term interest-only loan or an Option ARM (adjustable-rate mortgage) that minimizes the monthly payment if available. Otherwise select a 30 year fixed if that represents the lowest monthly payment. This will help you determine whether or nor you're buying the property at the right price. Obviously, you'll have a negative cash flow if you pay too much for the property. Then your Realtor® might suggest that you increase your down payment to produce a break-even cash flow. My advice is simply this: Don't do it! It's wiser to find another agent or at least focus on a different property. And this is key: Be prepared to buy in *other areas of the country* if property where you live is overpriced.

To illustrate, let's take a look at a recent typical transaction. All transactions in the primary category are similar, dealing with single-family detached homes, townhouses or condos. The scenario is different if you buy a duplex, triplex or a fourplex, but let's concentrate on our most common transaction: Example of a purchase of a $140,000 single-family home with 10% down

Although the above example is typical of the property I recommend, the whole story needs to be told. There are areas of the country where you can buy inexpensive property, such as the one listed above. But I *never* buy a property simply because it's cheap. That mindset will get you into trouble. You'll end up with cheap property and undesirable tenants. Not a good idea!

I'm very picky when it comes to choosing locations because, as I mentioned before, I want to attract the highest caliber of tenants. Therefore, I must purchase the best property in the best locations. I want NEW property that I can buy directly from the builder, but the purchase must be in a city or area that's projected to grow *at least 10%* a year for the next five years.

As with any other investment, you must do your homework first or have someone you trust do it for you. At S.C. Marketing, Inc. (*www.scm-inc.net*), we're constantly looking for property to buy for ourselves and our clients. We have a credible reputation with builders and Realtors®, who know that we're serious buyers and always in the market to purchase the right property.

Working with individual investors and corporate clients, we follow a disciplined approach to investing because we expect a high return annually along with the tax benefits. With a predictable 10% down payment and a 10% annual appreciation, we're earning 100% per year on our real estate investments. We may get that for two, three or more years, but we'll take it for as long as it lasts. We don't sell our property to capture any capital gain and pay taxes on it. Instead, we refinance in order to reap the myriad benefits of ever-growing equity.

Once we find the right property and make a purchase, it becomes part of our estate and will be passed along to our children and grandchildren. The property will eventually go into a trust to provide financial security for our families for generations. My children and grandchildren will never have to worry about a place to live or how to pay for their education. Never!

The equity in your real estate portfolio is your "personal bank," which represents a large portion of your net worth. You can always borrow against it. With thousands or millions of dollars in equity, you can go to your bank and get a secured line of credit to pay for your children's education or buy another property.

Don't use your line of credit buy a car or pay off credit cards. Vehicles begin depreciating the moment you buy them. The same is true for furniture and other items you need for your home. And forget about writing off the interest from your credit cards as a motivation to use your home equity line of credit. You have enough write-offs from your property.

I suggest that you use your equity line of credit for investment purposes only, such as buying more property or to invest in your children's future by paying for their education. Never buy depreciable assets with your credit line. Only invest in things that will appreciate because of "inflation".

Your children's education becomes an asset for them and will increase in value the more they use it. Bear in mind that your tenants will end up paying off your mortgage *and* your equity line of credit, so in fact your tenants are paying for your children's education.

As an incentive to your children to graduate from college, you might offer one of your properties (the one you borrowed against) as a gift upon successful completion of their studies. Now your children have starter properties that can be used to educate them on the investment strategies discussed in this book—strategies you've made your own through the process of building an estate. They don't teach it in college but they do teach sex education. I guess the colleges believe that sex is more important than financial security but an irresponsible financial status is the cause of more divorces than lack of sexual compatibility. But then, irresponsibility is acceptable behavior for many college professors in the mostly liberal agendas which is the primary reason for tenure. Lack of business savvy by college professors is not programmed into their DNA...they just deteriorate by degrees.

Your children now have a college education and own their first homes. They can live in it or continue to rent it. Either way, you must teach them how they can build an estate for themselves using the principles that helped you acquire your estate. Remember the biblical verse: "You can give a man a fish and feed him for a day, but TEACH a man to fish and you feed him for a lifetime." By the time your children are on their own, you'll have equipped with the wisdom that is contained in this book. The principles are ageless and know no boundaries.

As we become an increasingly global economy, your children may buy property in other countries and look for growth locations in other parts of the world. Owning real estate has always been a measure of wealth and, I predict, always will be.

Someday, owning land on another planet may provide financial security. When that happens, dust off this book and follow the same principles, because they're rooted in history and represent security regardless of one's rank or stature. Using OPM is, however, a uniquely sensible approach that may not be available for every investment and in every situation. As you're aware, leverage plays a major role important in improving your rate of return.

Always focus on the end result when you decide to invest in property. To have a positive and profitable experience, you must be able to attract the best tenants. There are tenants who could afford to buy their own home but prefer not to, and there are those who, for whatever reasons, aren't capable of purchasing their own home. I want to rent to the former rather than the latter. Having responsible tenants is critical for successful real estate investment. In most business ventures, your customers/clients/tenants ARE your business.

I am very upset when I hear a real estate agent tell me that they sold someone's house because the owner needed the equity (profit) to invest in a business. For some reason, the real estate agent didn't inform the home owner/seller that they are already in a business which has already created the profit that they want to use to invest in another business which has a higher chance of failure. Most new businesses fail in the first year. The real estate business also has a failure rate but is very small compared to other businesses. Wouldn't it make more sense to get a line of credit on the equity and buy more property? But, few real estate agents understand that logic. They are focused on getting the listing, doing open houses and selling the property in order to earn a commission. That's the primary reason that I am involved in training hundreds of real estate agents every month in the benefits and wisdom of "investing" in real estate and that it is a far safer investment than other business ventures and has far more business and tax benefits than any other business.

So, if real estate is the uncontested best investment, why don't more Realtors® invest in property? The simple truth is that few real estate agents understand investments, tax benefits, and how to select and structure an investment property. If you want to invest in real estate, you must first identify an agent who has extensive experience and success in this field.

Don't be afraid to put agents on the spot with key questions such as "How much property do you own?" and "What properties should I invest in and where?" If an agent encourages you to invest in what you perceive as overpriced properties and put more than 10% down to avoid a negative cash flow, it's time to continue looking. To get help locating an agent in your market, go to *www.TenPercentDown.com* and submit your request. You can also find suitable investment properties listed by states. For your information, we only work with and recommend agents who are educated by us and who really get it.

Back to the basics . . . If you faithfully follow the investment plan presented by this book, your real estate portfolio will continue to grow and provide financial security for your children and grandchildren. If you were to pay $1,000 for this book, you'd earn that back *10 times over* on your first purchase. It's even more remarkable, then, that your modest investment of $24.95 can create millions of dollars of profit and tax benefits not available through any other investment. After reading this book and understanding completely the principals contained herein, you will be disappointed if you attend any more seminars on real estate investing. You will also understand more about investing in real estate than 99% of all real estate agents. You will no longer buy into the stale advice being offered by other seminar leaders who encourage the purchase of books and tapes discussing no money down opportunities, foreclosures and fixer uppers, etc.

You now have the bottom-line knowledge to be a successful real state investor. Your experience and confidence will grow when you buy your first property using the principles presented in this book. As a helpful backup, you can also go to our corporate Website, *www.scm-*

inc.net, click on the "Investment Real Estate" page and send me your questions.

I urge you to create a practical and promising five-year plan, following every aspect of the advice I've shared on these pages. Start NOW!

AN IMPORTANT P.S.: *To help you locate the most desirable investment targets, we've created a robust Website where builders can post their new investment properties; buyers can search using specific parameters; Realtors® can identify homes to present to their clients; mortgage companies can offer various financing options; and property managers in many locations can advertise their services, such as advertising, renting and overseeing properties. It's an excellent, up-to-date, always evolving and improving resource. Log on to* www.TenPercentDown.com, *and you'll see what I mean!* This website is FREE and offers a monthly news letter.

Chapter 6

Confidence and Discipline

They're Keys to Your Investment Success

"Do or do not . . . There is no try." —*Yoda*

"Do it NOW. . ." —*W. Clement Stone*

"Why is that so important? Because procrastination is the art of failure before you begin." — Chuck Salisbury

How do you counteract the negative thinkers with whom you come into contact almost every day? The easiest way is to avoid them. Why add additional stress to your life and fight dragons you don't have to slay? What you do is *your* business. You don't need validation from others nor do you need their approval. While it's nice to be affirmed, never let the absence of other peoples' thumbs-up hold you back from doing the right thing.

Any experience can be beneficial—even if you tackle a problem and fail. You still gain experience and will know what to do differently next time. Of course, when you meet the challenge of a defining moment successfully, it will change your life.

Consider the great biblical story of David and Goliath. David's life was changed dramatically because of the challenge to slay a giant who was threatening and taunting the Israelite army. Goliath shouted that he would fight anyone in the army, with the outcome determining who would be victorious and who would go home in defeat. Not one soldier among the Israelites was willing to do battle with Goliath, so the king offered some very attractive incentives: his daughter in marriage, no taxes for the victor and his family, a new horse and more. David believed that he was chosen by God to save Israel and volunteered to slay the menacing giant.

Before the battle, David focused on the king's rewards, repeating to himself the generous offers and thereby creating a powerful picture of impending victory. He had complete confidence because he believed that his victory was God's will and that God would protect him.

David was victorious, and the battle changed his life. Eventually, he became the greatest king of Israel and ruled with the same confidence that led him to that life-shaping encounter with Goliath. Quite a journey—from a young shepherd to a dynastic ruler!

David had faith and confidence. But long before that defining moment, he was tested many times as a Shepard. He remarked how he had protected his flock against a bear and a lion. He was an accomplished marksman with a sling and a stone. He had been tested with smaller challenges and he constantly prevailed which helped to build his confidence. His faith was very real to him and he knew that if God was on his side then he could not fail because God was bigger than a thousand Goliath's. David was not born to kill Goliath but he was trained to fight that battle. When the time came he was ready and not one other person was. Thousands of soldiers prepared to go into battle against their counterparts and many knew that they would die. However, to a man, they were not ready to decide the fate of their country and they could not bring themselves to take a chance that might involve failure. No one wanted to be responsible for the defeat of Israel…except David. The only difference was that David focused on the rewards for the man who killed Goliath and never let the fear of failure detract him because of his enormous faith in himself and his God who had never abandoned him regardless of his past trials.

David had incredible faith and confidence. Again, just before going head to head with Goliath, he visualized himself riding on a new white horse, becoming a prince married to a princess and leading the people of Israel. He envisioned it, then he accomplished it!

Many of us fail to realize our goals because we're not confident enough and focus instead on the possibility of failure rather than the rewards of success. Life is a daily set of challenges and opportunities, and you'll be defined by how you respond to them. I used to give a talk titled "Goliath Was the Best Thing that Ever Happened to David." That says it all!

Many people would benefit by hearing the talk and, because it was recorded, you can purchase a tape or CD at my website. The other talk about persistence and overcoming adversity is called "Don't Give Up... Today Could Be The Day" and is also available at my website.

Confidence is key, of course, when it comes to investing in real estate. For most people, such investments are a total departure from their comfort level. People are comfortable investing in products offered by stock brokerage firms that often do nothing but make money for those companies. The stock firms are in the business of generating profits with OPM (other people's money). Their brokers are paid and rewarded based upon their personal production, not how well they manage your money.

As a former branch manager and trainer, I can assure you that nothing much has changed regarding the basic compensation package for brokers or agents of investment firms. Those who sell the most get paid the most. Whether you need it or not, whether you earn money or not, whether it benefits you or not, you will receive attention and service according to the *size* of your account. Brokers are offered certain incentives for selling company products rather than outside products such as outside Mutual Funds. The brokerage firms focus their attention on money under management and know how much income they can expect each broker to produce based upon how much money they have under management.

By sharp contrast, real estate is the *best investment* you can make, based upon past performances and future outlook—unless the rules change dramatically. As outlined in this book, investing in real estate is far ahead of any other investment and, as I noted in Chapter 1, there's no close second.

If you go to many real estate seminars, as I have, you'll get myriad opinions about the best ways to invest in property. Many seminars are conducted primarily to sell books, tapes and lengthy training sessions to separate you from your money. Save your money *and* your time! Most seminars are a rehash of old ideas and the seminar presenters know that it is easier to get a new audience rather than create a new seminar that is based upon the current real estate market. So they keep offering the same worn out advice (that doesn't work anymore but still sounds good) and continue to sell from a large warehouse of material. I have tried every method touted in the many seminars offered throughout America. Few work anywhere near what is promised. After 30 years of buying and selling real estate, as well as building apartments in bargain areas, I've developed a wealth-building program, presented by this book, that's consistently profitable and far less risky than most other investment tracks. I buy real estate to hold and never purchase property that doesn't attract high-quality tenants.

With my five-year plan, I'll refinance my properties, take out my original 10% DEPOSIT and continue to hold the property forever. Why? Because it remains quality real estate, and I have no money invested in it after I refinance. With the proceeds of a new 80% conforming loan, I'll be able to pocket enough money to buy two more properties so that my original 10% deposit has grown to the point that I'm able to own three properties—without adding more money to my investment. As the value of my properties grows, so does my equity. And it's the equity that allows me to keep buying more property without using my own money.

Your equity is your own "personal bank," because you're able to borrow against it and pledge that equity to secure your loan. What's more, the IRS allows you to depreciate your property even though its actual value continues to rise. Will it keep going up? Well, the average price of a single-family home in America has gone up every year since 1960, as I've noted already in the book. Does anyone think that the raw materials used to build a home are going to go down in price even though they continue to be in short supply? Check the prices of lumber, brick, cement and copper wire, then draw your own conclusions.

The basic commodity for home building is land. And as land prices continue to increase, so will the finished product. Based upon all the data included in this book, I'm comfortable with the conclusion that home prices will continue to increase. An obvious corollary is that rents will also continue to rise.

Back to the all-important issue of confidence . . . The more you know about real estate and about the facts supporting the conclusion that it's the best investment in the U.S., the more *confidence* you'll have about your decision to invest in this sector.

Are you aware that more fortunes have been made in real estate than any other financial/business pursuit? Knowledge is strength. Confidence comes from knowledge. Taking small steps to test what you know builds confidence. Therefore, buying one investment property becomes a confidence booster. If the experience is good, it leads you to buy a second, a third and so forth. Before you know it, you've built an estate, which leads you to take additional steps to protect those assets. (Your accountant may advise you to create a C corp. or an LLC [Limited Liability Corporation] to protect your assets and so they can be passed on to your children and grandchildren.)

All of this begins with a decision to buy a single investment property. Losing weight starts with a decision followed by a plan implemented with a lot of determination and discipline. Deciding to quit smoking is a similar process—one that exacts a price in terms of stress and effort, but one that can be enormously beneficial for a person's health as well.

Once you have the facts about the power of investment real estate to improve the *financial health* of you and your family, then you have to decide if you're willing to pay the price. The benefits are enormous and the results are conclusive and overwhelming. Losing weight, quitting smoking or becoming financially independent may be one of the Goliaths in your life. Especially with the last of those in mind, do you have the confidence and discipline to move forward? Are you up to the challenge?

Objectively, it's a lot easier than being overweight, being unable to walk or exercise because of ill health and certainly easier than retiring and being dependent upon the government and/or your family for the rest of your life.

I have made a few attempts to loose weight even though I am not greatly overweight. I am carrying enough weight to increase my blood pressure so it is not healthy. The weight I want to loose is around my waist which is the result of passing middle age. That's the time when the two middle's are obvious…middle age and middle tummy. The last time I tried to loose weight was through one of those new 30 day diets. The only thing I lost was a month. Now I am on a more credible diet called NutriSystem and I am following a disciplined approach that has proven very effective for thousands of people.

Chapter 7

"Invest" at Your Own Risk

When I was a stockbroker with Smith Barney in the early 80's I remember the T.V. ads that solemnly told listeners that we made money the "Old Fashion Way, We Earned It" . My fellow brokers and I mused over that slogan and immediately changed the wording to properly reflect the facts as we knew them. We never tired of exclaiming to each other, "We Make Money the Old Fashion Way, We Steal It". Those of us in the business knew better than our investors, clients and the gullible public. The stock brokerage firms are not in the business of making investors rich. They are not even in the business of making people money. This conclusion is based on nothing more than the facts. Most investors would be better off putting their money in an insured bank deposit making a modest yet secure return on their money and letting it compound. However, that is hardly an investment but is a better choice than most "investment" products offered by Stock Brokerage

Firms. In this book you will get the facts about Mutual Funds and the rate of return of other investment products.

You don't need to look far to affirm the conclusion that Stock Brokerage firms are in the business of making money for themselves and not for you. The firms that tout a diversified portfolio of secure, income producing investments are loaded with fees designed to produce a steady stream of income for the firm. Stockbrokers are paid commissions and the more money they raise and the more money they have under management the more they make. As a member of the "Chairman's Council or the President's Club" my awards were always based upon how much commissions I generated. The trips and other perks were based upon my production. When I was a branch manager I screened potential brokers with a test designed to measure their ability to sell products. I didn't want or need analytical guru's who were good at research and lengthy presentations on the merits of a particular stock or bond. The analyst wrote research reports and they were headquartered in New York. They produced the material that we used to "Sell" the products. We were never paid a penny based upon how well we served our clients. There was never an incentive for making money for the client...no contest to measure performance vs. production. I wasn't paid for exceptional results although I would have received more referrals if I was able to out perform the market. I paid my bills by selling products created by the firm designed to make money for the firm. The best products were those that attracted capital for the firm to manage over a long period of time with no liquidity. For the brokerage community it was all about managing "OPM" (Other Peoples Money). The biggest rip-off was and still is Mutual Funds and the results are outlined in this book. However, they are a big money maker for the firms that create them, manage them and sell them.

I would like for you to understand the basics of the Stock Market whether it be NASDAQ, NYSE or OTC. The price of the stock is determined by the Market Makers not the companies themselves. The companies may influence the price of their stock by establishing a consistent positive and profitable cash flow, issue timely news releases, hire a credible outside analyst to do a report on the companies attractive investment profile and hold regular "Road Shows" to attract new investors. The company can also be credited with keeping their existing stockholder informed on a regular basis. Every positive thing that the company does to encourage buying and discourage selling has a positive effect on the stock. Go to my website www.scm-inc.net to see what we offer to public companies that will help improve their stock's trading value.

Whenever I consulted with a public company I always credited a long term plan for growth that would encourage buying and discourage selling. I won't give up secrets on my methods but knowing the market and understanding why stocks increase in value is important to know if you want to make money by investing in stocks.

The first fact is that you don't make money in "the market". You make money by buying individual stocks. Before you buy you must do your homework and buy based upon facts not hype. Stockbrokers are paid commissions to hype stocks and their hype is supported by various research reports but often those reports are bias and were created specifically to promote buying which is designed to increase the stocks price. Unfortunately, it increases the price just long enough for the firm's large clients (hedge funds for example) to get out with a profit and then the price returns to its normal trading range. You are suckered in while the big boys are getting out. Firms also do that "Short Term Hype" so that they can clear their own position in a stock. The result is the Firm wins and the customer looses. Do they do that often? Of course they do. That's the business they're in. They are in the business of making money for themselves not you the customer. Of course they will take advantage of you. But what if you get unhappy and take your business elsewhere. Isn't that a concern to the large brokerage firms? Not really, because they know the transfer pattern and actually play to it. A customer will transfer from Smith Barney to Prudential or Merrill or another firm and the cycle continues. They keep using their profits to attract new money even if that money is already with another brokerage firm. Once you open an account with a new firm they will recommend ways to keep you long term such as put your money in Mutual Funds, Partnerships or with a Portfolio Manager so they can enjoy continuous cash flow from your money. Yes folks, it's all about keeping your money as long as possible so they can enjoy those "Trailer" fees for as long as possible. Should you invest with a broker who actually works hard to find good investments for you and actually makes money for you and keeps the fees at a minimum you should consider yourself lucky.

They deserve your praise because they are probably not getting it from their firm. They are probably not a member of the 'Chairman's Council" or "Presidents Club" etc. If he or she makes you money, take them out to lunch and you treat. They could probably use a good meal.

Chapter 8

Property Managers Are VIPs

*Or at Least They Should be in Your
Investment World*

My job is to buy property that I can rent to the best-qualified tenants, while a property manager's job is to find the best qualified tenants to occupy my property. When I identify and connect with a first-rate property manager, we're completely compatible and it's a win-win situation.

That said, I must alert you to the reality that finding competent, aggressive and professional property managers is a constant challenge. It's easier to find good properties than good property managers. Oftentimes real estate agents become property managers to create some stable cash flow between transactions. Still, their primary source of income is representing sellers and buyers of real property. They typically look at property management as an opportunity to create relationships with investors that will result in a listing and a large commission.

I don't recommend that you consider any Realtor® who's a part-time property manager. When agents are focused on bringing buyers and sellers together, they can use their financial resources to create self-serving opportunities at the expense of investors and their income properties. The net result frequently is a vacant property, which is the ultimate in negative cash flow.

As you've read in this book, I recommend that you never sell your property. Consequently, the opportunity for an agent to list my property or my client's property is nil. I strictly enforce the 10% rule regarding property management and never pay more than 10% of actual income. When the property is vacant, we both lose.

Bear in mind, too, that many real estate agents and some full-time property managers will depend on other agents to find a tenant for your property through an MLS listing. They try to minimize their out-of-pocket costs and avoid advertising your property in local print publications. Although every market is unique and may require different methods to locate qualified tenants, FULL-TIME property managers usually lead the way in innovation and creative ideas to accomplish the desired results.

Having a Website to post available property is a must for today's property managers. Advertising is designed to attract people looking for a home to rent, and truly effective ads include a Web address with the notation that many more properties are available. The best listing is featured to encourage people to visit the Website and then "register" exactly what they're looking for. The site must show pictures of the available property and highlight the details that will attract the right tenant and discourage unqualified prospects. (The properties I buy always have many builder upgrades to attract tenants, such as a patio, garage, garage-door opener, new washer and dryer, matching refrigerator, sliding shower door on any shower/tub combination and one-inch blinds on all windows so tenants will have immediate privacy upon move-in.)

As I've emphasized before, I make it a rule to buy/invest in the best homes in the best locations to attract the best possible tenants. While they're usually "entry level" homes, they're always new, and I buy directly from the builder. To reiterate what's already outlined in this book, I scout the country to find areas where I can expect an average annual growth of 10% for the first five years. This criterion has meant that I've passed on the opportunity to buy affordable homes in many markets that aren't growing. After all, I'm an investor, and I want growth as well as cash flow! I suggest that you honor the same principle in buying property.

The properties posted on my Website, *www.TenPercentDown.com*, have been identified as being in those growth areas. Use it as a resource to find property, property managers, research reports, and experienced and honest mortgage brokers. You'll discover that the site offers many other valuable investment tools as well.

OK, back to the selection of suitable property managers . . . I've included a copy of a management proposal that I received from a Realtor®/property manager so you can discover why this person effectively "excused himself" from the selection process. Under the proposal/contract is my e-mail response. You can see that I negotiate in good faith but will not violate the 10% rule that I talk about on my radio show and seminars. As I mentioned earlier, finding suitable property managers is an ongoing process, and I accept the responsibility to find them for you because I have the resources and leverage to negotiate the *best arrangement* for my buyers/investors.

When I locate potentially acceptable property managers (PMs), I negotiate by offering them at least 100 homes to manage if we come to terms. The PMs know I'm serious and that I can help them build their business. However, I'm firm about the 10% maximum fee arrangement. I'm at least thinking something like this: "If you want my business and that of my clients, then work hard and effectively within the guidelines that I establish. I don't give a rip about your current fee structure and your justification for charging more than 10%."

The bottom line: I make the offers, and the PMs take it or leave it. I've told my listeners and investors that if I have to, I'll start my own property management business in any area where we're investing if that's required to keep the costs to 10% while maintaining a high level of professionalism. Naming my property management company should be easy based on my proclivity for the word "Incredible." I think I'll call it the "Incredible Management Company." That seems to fit. Or I could call it the "10% Management Company."

Ah, another executive decision in the making. . . By the time you read this book, the decision will have been made. Understand that's it's not that I want to be in the PM business, but I simply won't abandon my principles or dishonor advice I give to others. So, out of necessity, I may create such a business to keep the PM fees to 10% as a prime benefit for my many new home investors.

How do you calculate the 10% and what does it include?

The simple rule is to annualize your property's income and take 10% of that. For example, if your rent is $1,000 per month or $12,000 per year, then the management fee must not exceed $1,200 annually. So if the property manager tells you that he or she has to pay one half of the first month's rent to another agent because the property was rented by that agent through the MLS, you subtract $500 from the annual allowable figure of $1,200—leaving $700 as a fee for the balance of the year. The remaining fee divided by 11 means that the monthly fee will be 6.36% for the rest of the year.

To enjoy the total 10% management fee, the PM must find a qualified tenant him- or herself and not depend on the MLS. Full-time PMs will be well-established and have a steady stream of prospects coming through their doors, while real estate agents often will depend on the MLS to find a tenant for your property.

Please note that the 10% management fee doesn't cover the additional costs of removing a tenant who fails to pay rent. Your lease contract should specify that the tenant will be charged for *all legal fees* incurred in the enforcement of the document. So, in addition to late fees and unpaid rent, the tenant will be charged all legal fees if the issue goes before the court. The tenant is also responsible for any damage to the property not covered by his or her security deposit. The lease contract should be for one year with an automatic month-to-month extension after that and an annual 5% rent increase on the anniversary date.

With such a contract, the PM won't have to renegotiate a new lease every year and charge you a fee for that effort. The good news is that the management fee is a simple 10% thereafter, which means the PM collects $1050, keeps $105 and sends the balance to you so you can pay your expenses.

In the lease I also add a late fee of $50 (5%) if the rent is not "received" by the PM by the 5th of the month. Forget the postmark!

The rent is unpaid if it's not in the hands of the PM by the 5th. If the PM hasn't received payment by the 10th, he or she begins the "Notice to Vacate" and whatever other legal steps are required to remove the tenant from your property. Again, the tenant then incurs further legal expenses, which are added to amount already due.

Always keep in mind that this is a business. It's your business, and you kept your part of the agreement when you purchased the property and added the many improvements to provide a quality home for someone to live in. The tenant must do his or her part by paying for the use of the home and doing so on time. Whether the tenant pays or not, your expenses must be covered every month. Take your business seriously and understand that tenants are your customers and that every one of them needs to be responsible.

I believe Will Rogers said it best when he stated, "I don't care about the return ON my investment until I understand the return OF my investment." Investing in real estate can be very rewarding, and you have a unique type of security—namely, the land itself. The "improvement" constructed on the land will age and may someday have to be replaced, but the underlying security is always the land. The land is ageless and underlies the strong, enduring assurance that you can never lose all your money—unlike in the stock market.

Investors who hear my radio show and attend my seminars often tell me that they don't want to have a negative cash flow on their income property. Then, after making a purchase, they'll tell their PM that they MUST rent their property for a charge that will cover their entire monthly expenses, including mortgage payment, taxes, insurance and the 10% management fee. It's essential to understand that the initial rental rate may not cover 100% of your expenses. Fortunately, since I suggest raising the rent 5% per year, you'll soon be able to "rise above" that negative cash flow.

Of course, when the PM shows your property but the prospective tenant rents a comparable home for a lower rent, your property remains vacant and that presents the biggest negative cash flow possible. So if you have a vacant property resulting from your initial insistence on covering 100% of your costs then you must rethink your objective to make money through a long term plan. If you've selected a good property manager, ask him or her what the rent should be for attracting a suitable tenant to *help pay* your monthly expenses. But beware of selecting a lazy PM who suggests a rent below the actual market rate simply to sign up a tenant quickly without having to show the property often. A lazy PM will cost you money. Show him or her the door ASAP!

Finally, who's a suitable tenant for your highly desirable, new single-family home? Insist on the following from your PM: Find tenants with good credit scores, call their current landlord and ask if they've paid their rent on time for the past 12 months; then do a background check to keep undesirable tenants from renting your property. My ideal tenant would be a small family where the husband works and the wife stays home with the children. The next option is where both work and the children are in school daily or they stay at a licensed child care provider. But reliable tenants are a key to your investment success, and that's why I've outlined a proven process for finding such tenants. The best tenant is the one who pays rent on time and takes care of the property as they would if they owned it.

Outline for standard MLS Rental/Lease Agreement...
Notice to the PM from us.

(TAR-2201) 10-5-05

Produced with ZipForm™ by RE FormsNet, LLC 18025 Fifteen Mile Road, Clinton Township, Michigan 48035 www.zipform.com

PROPERTY

Leasing & Management Agreement concerning: _____

    C. <u>Effective Services</u>: If Broker determines that Broker cannot continue to effectively provide leasing and management services to Owner for any reason at any time during this agreement Broker may terminate this agreement by providing at least 30 days written notice to Owner.

4. AUTHORITY OF BROKER:

    A. <u>Leasing and Management Authority</u>: Owner grants to Broker the following authority which Broker may exercise when and to the extent Broker determines to be in Owner's interest:

      (1) advertise the Property for lease at Owner's expense by means and methods that Broker determines are reasonably competitive, including but not limited to creating and placing advertisements with interior and exterior photographic and audio-visual images of the Property and related information in any media and the Internet;

      (2) place "For Lease" signs or other signs on the Property in accordance with applicable laws, regulations, ordinances, restrictions, and owners' association rules;

      (3) remove all other signs offering the Property for sale or lease;

      (4) submit the Property as a listing with one or more Multiple Listing Services (MLS) at any time the Property is marketed for lease and to change or terminate such listings;

      (5) authorize other brokers, their associates, inspectors, appraisers, and contractors to access the Property at reasonable times for purposes contemplated by this agreement and to lend keys and disclose security codes to such persons to enter the Property;

      (6) duplicate keys and access devices, at Owner's expense, to facilitate convenient and efficient showings of the Property and to lease the Property;

      (7) place a keybox on the Property;

      (8) employ scheduling companies to schedule showings by other brokers at any time the Property is marketed for lease;

      (9) verify information and references in rental applications from prospective tenants;

      (10) negotiate and execute leases on Owner's behalf for the Property at market rates and on competitively reasonable terms for initial terms of not less than _____ months and not more than _____ months and in accordance with any instructions in Paragraph 20;

      (11) negotiate and execute any amendments, extensions, or renewals to any leases for the Property on Owner's behalf;

      (12) terminate leases for the Property, negotiate lease terminations, and serve notices of termination;

      (13) collect and deposit for Owner rents, security deposits, and other funds related to the Property in a trust account and pay from that account: (a) any compensation and reimbursements due Broker under this agreement; and (b) other persons as this agreement may authorize.

      (14) account for security deposits that Broker holds in trust to any tenants in the Property in accordance with applicable law and any lease of the Property and make deductions from the deposits in accordance with the lease and applicable law;

      (15) collect administrative charges including but not limited to, application fees, returned check fees, and late charges from tenants in the Property or from prospective tenants;

      (16) institute and prosecute, at Owner's expense, actions to: (a) evict tenants in the Property; (b) recover possession of the Property; or (c) recover lost rent and other damages;

      (17) settle, compromise, or withdraw any action described in Paragraph 4A(16);

      (18) negotiate and make reasonable concessions to tenants or former tenants in the Property;

      (19) report payment histories of tenants in the Property to consumer reporting agencies;

      (20) obtain information from any holder of a note secured by a lien on the Property and any insurance company insuring all or part of the Property;

      (21) hire contractors to repair, maintain, redecorate, or alter the Property provided that Broker does not expend more than $ _____ for any single repair, maintenance item, redecoration, or alteration without Owner's consent;

      (22) hire contractors to make emergency repairs to the Property without regard to the expense limita-

(TAR-2201) 10-5-05 Initialed for Identification by: Broker/Associate_____ and Owner _____ , _____   Page 2 of 11

Produced with ZipForm™ by RE FormsNet, LLC 18025 Fifteen Mile Road, Clinton Township, Michigan 48035 www.zipform.com   PROPERTY

64

tion in Paragraph 4A(21) that Broker determines are necessary to protect the Property or the health or safety of an ordinary tenant;

(23) contract, at Owner's expense, for utilities and maintenance to the Property during times that the Property is vacant, including but not limited to, electricity, gas, water, alarm monitoring, cleaning, pool and spa maintenance, yard maintenance, and other regularly recurring expenses that Broker determines are reasonable to maintain and care for the Property; and

(24) perform other necessary services related to the leasing and management of the Property.

B. Record Keeping: Broker will:
   (1) maintain accurate records related to the Property and retain such records for not less than 4 years;
   (2) file reports with the Internal Revenue Service related to funds received on behalf of Owner under this agreement (for example, Form 1099); and
   (3) remit, each month, the following items to Owner at the address specified in Paragraph 1: (a) funds collected by Broker for Owner under this agreement, less authorized deductions; and (b) a statement of receipts, disbursements, and charges. Owner may instruct Broker in writing to remit the items to another person or address.

C. Security Deposits:
   (1) During this agreement, Broker will maintain security deposits received from tenants in a trust account and will account to the tenants for the security deposits in accordance with the leases for the Property.
   (2) After this agreement ends, Broker will deliver to Owner or the Owner's designee the security deposit held by Broker under an effective lease of the Property, less deductions authorized by this agreement, and will send written notice to the tenant that states:
       (a) that this agreement has ended;
       (b) the exact dollar amount of the security deposit;
       (c) the contact information for the Owner or the Owner's designee; and
       (d) that Owner is responsible for accounting for and returning the tenant's security deposit.
   (3) If Broker complies with this Paragraph 4C, Owner will indemnify Broker from any claim or loss from a tenant for the return of a security deposit. This Paragraph 4C survives termination of this agreement.

D. Performance Standard: Broker will:
   (1) use reasonable care when exercising Broker's authority and performing under this agreement; and
   (2) exercise discretion when performing under this agreement in a manner that Broker believes to be in Owner's interest, provided that Broker will treat any tenant honestly and fairly.

E. Deductions and Offset: Broker may disburse from any funds Broker holds in a trust account for Owner:
   (1) any compensation due Broker under this agreement;
   (2) any funds Broker is authorized to expend under this agreement; and
   (3) any reimbursement Broker is entitled to receive under this agreement.

F. Insurance and Attorneys:
   (1) Broker may not file a claim for a casualty loss with the carrier insuring the Property. Broker may communicate with the carrier to facilitate the processing of any claim Owner may file or other matters that Owner instructs Broker to communicate to the carrier.
   (2) Broker may not directly or indirectly employ or pay a lawyer to represent Owner. Broker may communicate with Owner's attorney in accordance with Owner's instructions.

G. Information about Trust Accounts, MLS, and Keybox:
   (1) Trust Accounts: A trust account must be separate from Broker's operating account and must be designated as a trust, property management, or escrow account or other similar name. Broker may maintain one trust account for all properties Broker leases and manages for others.

(TAR-2201) 10-5-05 Initialed for Identification by: Broker/Associate _____ and Owner _____ , _____   Page 3 of 11

Produced with ZipForm™ by RE FormsNet, LLC 18025 Fifteen Mile Road, Clinton Township, Michigan 48035 www.zipform.com   PROPERTY

Leasing & Management Agreement concerning: _____

(2) <u>MLS</u>: MLS rules require Broker to accurately and timely submit all information the MLS requires for participation including leased data. Subscribers to the MLS may use the information for market evaluation or appraisal purposes. Subscribers are other brokers and other real estate professionals such as appraisers and may include the appraisal district. Any information filed with the MLS becomes the property of the MLS for all purposes. *Submission of information to MLS ensures that persons who use and benefit from the MLS also contribute information.*

(3) <u>Keybox</u>: A keybox is a locked container placed on the Property that holds a key to the Property. A keybox makes it more convenient for brokers, their associates, inspectors, appraisers, and contractors to show, inspect, or repair the Property. The keybox is opened by a special combination, key, or programmed device, so that authorized persons may enter the Property. Using a keybox will probably increase the number of showings, but involves risks (for example, unauthorized entry, theft, property damage, or personal injury). *Neither the Association of REALTORS® nor MLS requires the use of a keybox.*

5. **LEGAL COMPLIANCE:** The parties will comply with all obligations, duties, and responsibilities under the Texas Property Code, fair housing laws, and any other statute, administrative rule, ordinance, or restrictive covenant applicable to the use, leasing, management, or care of the Property.

6. **RESERVES:** Upon execution of this agreement, Owner will deposit the following amount with Broker to be held in a trust account as a reserve for Owner: $ _____ for each unit within the Property or Properties managed by Broker under this agreement. Broker may, at Broker's discretion, use the reserve to pay any expense related to the leasing and management of the Property(ies) (including but not limited to Broker's fees). If the balance of the reserve becomes less than the amount stated, at any time, Broker may: (a) deduct an amount that will bring the balance to the amount stated from any subsequent rent received on behalf of Owner and deposit the amount into the reserve; or (b) notify Owner that Owner must promptly deposit additional funds with Broker to bring the balance to the amount stated.

7. **ADVANCES:** Owner will, in advance, provide Broker all funds necessary for the leasing and management of the Property. Broker is not obligated to advance any money to Owner or to any other person.

8. **OWNER'S REPRESENTATIONS:**

A. <u>General</u>:
(1) Except as disclosed in Paragraph 20, Owner represents that:
   (a) Owner has fee simple title to and peaceable possession of the Property and all its improvements and fixtures, unless rented, and the legal capacity to lease the Property;
   (b) Owner is not bound by: (i) another agreement with another broker for the sale, exchange, lease, or management of the Property that is or will be in effect during this agreement; or (ii) an agreement or covenant that prohibits owner from leasing the property;
   (c) no person or entity has any right to purchase, lease, or acquire the Property by an option, right of refusal, or other agreement;
   (d) Owner is not delinquent in the payment of any property taxes, owners' association fees, property insurance, mortgage, or any encumbrance on or affecting the Property;
   (e) the Property is not subject to the jurisdiction of any court;
   (f) the optional user fees for the use of common areas (for example, pool or tennis courts) in the Property's subdivision are: _____ ; and
   (g) all information related to the Property that Owner provides to Broker is true and correct to the best of Owner's knowledge.

(2) Broker may disclose to a tenant or to a prospective tenant any information related to the representations made in this Paragraph 9.

(TAR-2201) 10-5-05 Initialed for Identification by: Broker/Associate_____ and Owner _____ : _____   Page 4 of 11

Produced with ZipForm™ by RE FormsNet, LLC 18025 Fifteen Mile Road, Clinton Township, Michigan 48035 www.zipform.com   PROPERTY

Leasing & Management Agreement concerning: _____

    (1) purchase insurance that will provide Broker the same coverage as the required insurance under Paragraph 10A(1) and Owner must promptly reimburse Broker for such expense; or

    (2) exercise Broker's remedies under Paragraph 17.

11. BROKER'S FEES: All fees to Broker under this agreement are payable in _____ County, Texas. This Paragraph 11 survives termination or expiration of this agreement with regard to fees earned during this agreement which are not payable until after its termination. Broker may deduct any fees under this Paragraph 11 from any funds Broker holds in trust for Owner. If more than one property or unit is made part of and subject to this agreement, each of the provisions below will apply to each property or unit separately.

❏ A. Management Fees: Each month Owner will pay Broker the greater of $ _____ (minimum management fee) or: (Check one box only.)

    ❏ (1) _____ % of the gross monthly rents collected that month.

    ❏ (2) _____

    A vacancy in the Property or failure by a tenant to pay rent does not excuse payment of the minimum management fee. Management fees under this Paragraph 11A are earned daily and are payable not later than the last day of each month.

❏ B. Leasing Fees for New Tenancies: Each time the Property is leased to a new tenant, Owner will pay Broker a leasing fee equal to: (Check one box only.)

    ❏ (1) _____ % of one full month's rent to be paid under the lease.

    ❏ (2) _____ % of the gross rents to be paid under the lease.

    ❏ (3) _____

    The leasing fees under this Paragraph 11B are earned and payable at the time the lease is executed.

❏ C. Renewal or Extension Fees: Each time a tenant in the Property renews or extends a lease, Owner will pay Broker a renewal or extension fee equal to: (Check one box only.)

    ❏ (1) _____ % of one full month's rent to be paid under the renewal or extension.

    ❏ (2) _____ % of the gross rents to be paid under the renewal or extension.

    ❏ (3) _____

    The renewal or extension fees under this Paragraph 11C are earned and payable at the time the renewal or extension is effective. For the purposes of this paragraph, a new lease for the same Property with the same tenant then occupying the Property is an extension or renewal. This Paragraph 11C does not apply to month-to-month renewals or month-to-month extensions.

❏ D. Service Fees: Each time Broker arranges for the Property to be repaired, maintained, redecorated, or altered as permitted by this agreement, Owner will pay Broker a service fee equal to: (Check one box only.)

    ❏ (1) _____ % of the total cost of each repair, maintenance, alteration, or redecoration.

    ❏ (2) _____

    The service fees under this Paragraph 11D are earned at the time the repair, maintenance, redecoration, or alteration is made and are payable upon Owner's receipt of Broker's invoice.

❏ E. Interest on Trust Accounts: Any trust account Broker maintains under this agreement may be an interest-bearing or income producing account. Broker may retain any interest or income from such account as compensation under this agreement. Broker will remove any interest or income payable under this Paragraph 11E from the trust account not later than the 30th day after the interest or income is paid.

❏ F. Administrative Fees: If Broker collects administrative charges from tenants or prospective tenants, including but not limited to, application fees, returned check fees, or late charges (as authorized under Paragraph 4A), Broker will retain such fees as compensation under this agreement. The administrative fees under this Paragraph 11F are earned and payable at the time Broker collects such fees.

(TAR-2201) 10-5-05 Initialed for Identification by: Broker/Associate_____ and Owner _____ , _____   Page 6 of 11

Produced with ZipForm™ by RE FormsNet, LLC 18025 Fifteen Mile Road, Clinton Township, Michigan 48035 www.zipform.com   PROPERTY

67

    (1) purchase insurance that will provide Broker the same coverage as the required insurance under Paragraph 10A(1) and Owner must promptly reimburse Broker for such expense; or

    (2) exercise Broker's remedies under Paragraph 17.

11. BROKER'S FEES: All fees to Broker under this agreement are payable in _____ County, Texas. This Paragraph 11 survives termination or expiration of this agreement with regard to fees earned during this agreement which are not payable until after its termination. Broker may deduct any fees under this Paragraph 11 from any funds Broker holds in trust for Owner. If more than one property or unit is made part of and subject to this agreement, each of the provisions below will apply to each property or unit separately.

❏ A. Management Fees: Each month Owner will pay Broker the greater of $ _____ (minimum management fee) or: *(Check one box only.)*
    ❏ (1) _____ % of the gross monthly rents collected that month.
    ❏ (2) _____
    A vacancy in the Property or failure by a tenant to pay rent does not excuse payment of the minimum management fee. Management fees under this Paragraph 11A are earned daily and are payable not later than the last day of each month.

❏ B. Leasing Fees for New Tenancies: Each time the Property is leased to a new tenant, Owner will pay Broker a leasing fee equal to: *(Check one box only.)*
    ❏ (1) _____ % of one full month's rent to be paid under the lease.
    ❏ (2) _____ % of the gross rents to be paid under the lease.
    ❏ (3) _____
    The leasing fees under this Paragraph 11B are earned and payable at the time the lease is executed.

❏ C. Renewal or Extension Fees: Each time a tenant in the Property renews or extends a lease, Owner will pay Broker a renewal or extension fee equal to: *(Check one box only.)*
    ❏ (1) _____ % of one full month's rent to be paid under the renewal or extension.
    ❏ (2) _____ % of the gross rents to be paid under the renewal or extension.
    ❏ (3) _____
    The renewal or extension fees under this Paragraph 11C are earned and payable at the time the renewal or extension is effective. For the purposes of this paragraph, a new lease for the same Property with the same tenant then occupying the Property is an extension or renewal. This Paragraph 11C does not apply to month-to-month renewals or month-to-month extensions.

❏ D. Service Fees: Each time Broker arranges for the Property to be repaired, maintained, redecorated, or altered as permitted by this agreement, Owner will pay Broker a service fee equal to: *(Check one box only.)*
    ❏ (1) _____ % of the total cost of each repair, maintenance, alteration, or redecoration.
    ❏ (2) _____
    The service fees under this Paragraph 11D are earned at the time the repair, maintenance, redecoration, or alteration is made and are payable upon Owner's receipt of Broker's invoice.

❏ E. Interest on Trust Accounts: Any trust account Broker maintains under this agreement may be an interest-bearing or income producing account. Broker may retain any interest or income from such account as compensation under this agreement. Broker will remove any interest or income payable under this Paragraph 11E from the trust account not later than the 30th day after the interest or income is paid.

❏ F. Administrative Fees: If Broker collects administrative charges from tenants or prospective tenants, including but not limited to, application fees, returned check fees, or late charges (as authorized under Paragraph 4A), Broker will retain such fees as compensation under this agreement. The administrative fees under this Paragraph 11F are earned and payable at the time Broker collects such fees.

(TAR-2201) 10-5-05 Initialed for Identification by: Broker/Associate _____ and Owner _____   Page 6 of 11

Produced with ZipForm™ by RE FormsNet, LLC 18025 Fifteen Mile Road, Clinton Township, Michigan 48035 www.zipform.com   PROPERTY

68

Leasing & Management Agreement concerning: _____

❏ G. **Fees Related to Insurance and Legal Matters:** If Owner requests or instructs Broker to coordinate or communicate with any insurance carrier regarding any casualty to or on the Property or if Owner requests or instructs Broker to appear in any legal proceeding or deposition related to the Property (including, but not limited to, evictions, tenant disputes, security deposit disputes, and suits for damages), Owner will pay Broker $_____ per _____ for Broker's time expended in such matters and in preparation of such matters. Fees under this Paragraph 11G are earned at the time the services are rendered and payable upon Owner's receipt of Broker's invoice.

❏ H. **Fees in the Event of a Sale:**

    (1) **Fee if a Tenant Purchases Property:** If at any time during this agreement or within _____ days after it ends, Owner sells the Property to a tenant who occupied the Property during the term of this agreement, Owner will pay Broker a fee equal to: *(Check one box only.)*
    ❏ (a) _____ % of the sales price.
    ❏ (b) _____ .
    Fees under this Paragraph 11H(1) are earned at the time Owner agrees to sell the Property and are payable at the time the sale closes. Broker will waive any fees due under Paragraph 12 at the time the sale closes.

    (2) **Fee if Buyer is Procured through Broker:** If during this agreement, Owner agrees to sell the Property to a person other than a tenant who occupied the Property and Broker procures the buyer, directly or through another broker, Owner will pay Broker a fee equal to: *(Check one box only.)*
    ❏ (a) _____ % of the sales price.
    ❏ (b) _____ .
    Fees under this Paragraph 11H(2) are earned at the time Owner agrees to sell the Property and are payable at the time the sale closes. Broker will waive any fees due under Paragraph 12 at the time the sale closes.

    (3) **Sale Coordination Fees:** If at any time during this agreement Owner agrees to sell the Property and Broker is not paid a fee under Paragraph 11H(1) or (2), Owner will pay Broker _____ _____ for Broker's time and services to coordinate showings, inspections, appraisals, repairs, and other related matters. Fees under this Paragraph 11H(3) are earned at the time such services are rendered and payable upon Owner's receipt of Broker's invoice.

    (4) **Definition:** "Sell" means to agree to sell, convey, transfer or exchange any interest in the Property whether by oral or written agreement or option.

    (5) **Separate Listing Agreement Controls:** If Owner sells the Property and pays Broker the fee under a separate written listing agreement between Owner and Broker: (a) this Paragraph 11H will not apply; and (b) Broker will waive any fees due under Paragraph 12 at the time the sale closes.

❏ I. **Other:** _____
    _____
    _____

12. FEES UPON TERMINATION: At the time this agreement ends, Owner must pay Broker:
    A. all amounts due Broker under this agreement; and
    B. if the Property is leased to a tenant on the date this agreement ends and Owner terminates this agreement, an amount equal to the lesser of:
        (a) the management fees that would accrue over the remainder of the term of the lease; or
        (b) $_____ .
    If more than one property or unit is made part of and subject to this agreement, this paragraph applies only to those properties or units then leased and applies to each property or unit separately.

(TAR-2201) 10-5-05 Initialed for Identification by: Broker/Associate_____ and Owner _____ , _____   Page 7 of 11
Produced with ZipForm™ by RE FormsNet, LLC 18025 Fifteen Mile Road, Clinton Township, Michigan 48035 www.zipform.com   PROPERTY

69

Leasing & Management Agreement concerning: _____

C. Owner agrees to protect, defend, indemnify, and hold Broker harmless from any damage, costs, attorney's fees, and expenses that:
   (1) are caused by Owner, negligently or otherwise;
   (2) arise from Owner's failure to disclose any material or relevant information about the Property;
   (3) are caused by Owner giving incorrect information to any person; or
   (4) are related to the management of the Property and are not caused by Broker, negligently or otherwise.

D. Owner is responsible and liable for all contracts and obligations related to the Property (for example, maintenance, service, repair and utility agreements) entered into before or during this agreement by Owner or by Broker under Broker's authority under this agreement. Owner agrees to hold Broker harmless from all claims related to any such contracts.

17. **DEFAULT:** A party is in default if the party fails to cure a breach within 10 days after receipt of written demand from the other party. If either party is in default, the non-defaulting party may: (a) terminate this agreement by providing at least 10 days written notice; (b) recover all amounts due to the non-defaulting party under this agreement; (c) recover reasonable collection costs and attorney's fees; and (d) exercise any other remedy available at law. Broker is also entitled to recover any compensation Broker would have been entitled to receive if Owner did not breach this agreement.

18. **MEDIATION:** The parties agree to negotiate in good faith in an effort to resolve any dispute related to this agreement that may arise between the parties. If the dispute cannot be resolved by negotiation, the dispute will be submitted to mediation. The parties to the dispute will choose a mutually acceptable mediator and will share the cost of mediation equally.

19. **ATTORNEY'S FEES:** If Owner or Broker is a prevailing party in any legal proceeding brought as a result of a dispute under this agreement or any transaction related to or contemplated by this agreement, such party will be entitled to recover from the non-prevailing party all costs of such proceeding and reasonable attorney's fees.

20. **SPECIAL PROVISIONS:**

21. **ADDENDA:** Incorporated into this agreement are the following addenda, exhibits, and other information:
   ☑ A. Information About Brokerage Services
   ❑ B. Addendum Regarding Lead-Based Paint
   ❑ C. Multiple Property Addendum
   ❑ D. Owner's Notice Concerning Condition of Property under Property Management Agreement
   ❑ E. Property Manager's Inventory and Condition Report
   ❑ F. Addendum for Authorization to Act for Owner before Owners' Association
   ❑ G. Copy of Rules and Regulations of an Owners' Association
   ❑ H. Copy of the Owners' Association Bylaws and Deed Restrictions affecting the Property
   ❑ I. _____

Note: Complete and deliver to Broker IRS W-9 Form or similar form. Broker maintains a privacy policy that is available upon request.

(TAR-2201) 10-5-05 Initialed for Identification by: Broker/Associate_____ and Owner _____ . _____   Page 9 of 11

Produced with ZipForm™ by RE FormsNet, LLC 18025 Fifteen Mile Road, Clinton Township, Michigan 48035 www.zipform.com   PROPERTY

Leasing & Management Agreement concerning: _____

22. AGREEMENT OF PARTIES:

A. Entire Agreement: This document contains the entire agreement of the parties and may not be changed except by written agreement.

B. Assignments: Neither party may assign this agreement without the written consent of the other party.

C. Binding Effect: Owner's obligation to pay Broker an earned fee is binding upon Owner and Owner's heirs, administrators, executors, successors, and permitted assignees.

D. Joint and Several: All Owners executing this agreement are jointly and severally liable for the performance of all its terms. Any act or notice to, refund to, or signature of, any one or more of the Owners regarding any term of this agreement, its extension, its renewal, or its termination is binding on all Owners executing this agreement.

E. Governing Law: Texas law governs the interpretation, validity, performance, and enforcement of this agreement.

F. Severability: If a court finds any clause in this agreement invalid or unenforceable, the remainder of this agreement will not be affected and all other provisions of this agreement will remain valid and enforceable.

G. Context: When the context requires, singular nouns and pronouns include the plural.

H. Notices: Notices between the parties must be in writing and are effective when sent to the receiving party's address, fax, or e-mail address specified in Paragraph 1.

23. INFORMATION:

A. **Broker's fees or the sharing of fees between brokers are not fixed, controlled, recommended, suggested, or maintained by the Association of REALTORS®, MLS, or any listing service.**

B. **Fair housing laws require the Property to be shown and made available to all persons without regard to race, color, religion, national origin, sex, disability, or familial status. Local ordinances may provide for additional protected classes (for example, creed, status as a student, marital status, sexual orientation, or age).**

C. **Owner may review the information Broker submits to an MLS or other listing service.**

D. **Broker advises Owner to remove or secure jewelry, prescription drugs, and other valuables.**

E. **The Property Code requires certain types of locks or security devices on all exterior doors of residential rental properties and requires smoke detectors in certain locations. The Property Code requires the security devices to be rekeyed and the smoke detectors to be tested each time a new tenant occupies the Property.**

F. **Broker cannot give legal advice. READ THIS AGREEMENT CAREFULLY. If you do not understand the effect of this agreement, consult an attorney BEFORE signing.**

Broker's Printed Name	License No.	Owner
By: _____		By: _____
Broker's Associate's Signature	Date	Date
		Owner
		By: _____
		Date

(TAR-2201) 10-5-05

Produced with ZipForm™ by RE FormsNet, LLC 18025 Fifteen Mile Road, Clinton Township, Michigan 48035 www.zipform.com

Leasing & Management Agreement concerning: _____

Index to Residential Leasing and Property Management Agreement

(TAR-2201) 10-5-05

Produced with ZipForm™ by RE FormsNet, LLC 18025 Fifteen Mile Road, Clinton Township, Michigan 48035 www.zipform.com

Page 11 of 11

PROPERTY

72

Thanks for your email. Yes, I am buying a lot of property in your area and would like to have a Great property manager (PM). After reviewing the contract you submitted (attached), you must make the following changes in order to get my free referrals. First, delete the $1,000. fee on page 4 for reserves. We only buy new property and any maintenance issues are referred to the builder to be corrected. Under insurance (page 5), my clients provide liability insurance necessary to repair their property if a claim is required because of some damage. You must provide your own E & O insurance in order to be in business and the liability, should any arise, is your cost of doing business. On page 6 the management Fee of 10% is agreed upon but there cannot be an additional fee of 80% of the first months rent to be paid as a leasing fee.

The TOTAL compensation must not exceed 10% of the annual rental income. You can divide it as you see fit if you involve the MLS. Also, Rental agreements are for a period of one year and then automatically convert to month to month with an automatic 5% rent increase on the anniversary date. From the anniversary date forward the tenant may terminate with a 30 day notice. The Property Manager will conduct a walk-through prior to the start of the lease and before the tenant moves to determine what portion of their security deposit is refundable. The security deposit is always one months rent payable before move-in and the first months rent payable with a cashiers check or money order just prior to move-in.

Delete anything related to the SALE of the property (page 7) as there will never be a sale. We are buyers and do not intend to sale. Under termination (Item 12) there should be no fees due as you will collect/receive the rent monthly and subtract the amount that is due for management. The property management agreement is for a one year period and also reverts to month to month thereafter with a 30 notice necessary to cancel. Item 14 should not happen if the tenant is properly informed that a new property manager has been selected and rent payments will be mailed to the new PM. In the event that a tenant mails their payment to the wrong address the check must be immediately forwarded to the right PM. If you can review and acknowledge your agreement to these terms then you can have a free banner on my website www.tenpercentdown.com and should therefore receive the property management business for at least 100 properties a year.

Chapter 9

Where Do You Buy?

The Search for a 10% Growth Market.

All successful investments begin with a plan and action steps designed to support your objective. The more time you put in to finding the right investment the more experience you'll get and, like all other things in life, you will get better at finding the right investment opportunities. Making mistakes is part of the process because there is no perfect process or perfect investment. People are different, investments are different and results vary over time because markets shift and what worked yesterday might not work the same next time. So, being adaptive and flexible is important when searching for the right place to invest your money. Realators truthfully say that you make money when you buy and you see the results when you sell. How true.

Looking for a growth area in Real Estate is no different. I will share with you the way I look for undervalued markets so that you can mimic me or use my experience as a resource to add value to whatever you're doing. My initial goals are to locate areas of the U.S. where growth is almost predictable because certain infrastructure investments have already been made. Growth areas are identified by new roads or widening existing ones to handle increased traffic. Usually the growth areas are suburban as an established and aging community finds its citizen looking for better schools, better shopping and newer recreation facilities. Corporate America also searches for urban flight and growth to determine where they are going to expand and build those new Super stores. County governments usually lead the way by identifying urban areas that are primed to grow and fund newly created Redevelopment areas that will include new roads, freeways, industrial parks, schools and master planning to attract major retailers and businesses. In looking for growth that will support my 10% property appreciation objective, I am a follower not a leader. Corporate America and local governments determine what will be and create those growth markets that I seek.

You can find these markets through various ways including reading national publications like Forbes and Fortune that identify growth trends and publish lists of the 10 Hottest Urban growth markets or the best place to retire, etc. Many other publications will identify growth areas. I occasionally receive tips from residents of a local area that tell me about all the activity going on in their community. When you live in a growth area you can't help but know it. You can see and experience the growth. If you don't live in a growth area but want to locate them you can find out where Wal Mart and Kmart are building their new Super Centers or find out where those new building supply houses are locating new stores. Lowes doesn't build large stores to sell building supplies unless there is a need. Using common sense and knowing what to look for will be important in your search for growth markets. The final test for me is an actual visit to the area. That may require a plane trip and an overnight trip. Go there, rent a car and travel the area. Talk to local residents and businesses and ask about plans for the future. The local residents know what is being planned by reading their local newspaper. It costs money to do research but the reward will be a pay back for many years to come. On my website I offer research reports on any area that we are buying in and those that we are investigating. This is a free resource if you register at www.TenPercentDown.com.

Because the demographics of all areas will change over time it is always advisable to return to the TenPercentDown website to locate the new areas of interest and see a selection of homes in the 10% growth areas. Also, the tax benefits may change over time. Despite the fact that you are only putting 10% down payment and using 90% of other peoples money (OPM), you enjoy 100% of the tax benefits. For example you can depreciate your investment property over 27.5 years (not the land), deduct the interest on your mortgage loan and the property taxes paid every year. Additional expenses such as repairs and the 10% property management fee is also a tax benefit.

People, like yourself, who want to enjoy the benefits of real estate ownership are often tempted to attend real estate seminars advertised with large newspaper ads or slick mailing programs. Are they any good and will they help you make money in real estate? I have a test that you can use to avoid wasting money on seminars that promise more than they can deliver and actually waste your money and cause more harm than good. The tip-off is during the closing sessions of these FREE seminars. you will determine the real reason why the speaker and his/her company is providing these free or teaser seminars. Near the conclusion they start talking about the course that they are offering and how valuable it is. They will put an artificial value on the course and then offer a special discount if you sign-up there and then. At that point you should get up and leave.

I've had people attend my seminar and tell me that they were offered real estate courses for $5,000. that will teach them how to make a "Fortune in Foreclosures". The only people that make the money are the ones offering the course. The same can be said about Estate Sales, Distressed or Fixer Uppers. There are T.V. programs glamorizing the role of "simple folk" who can "flip" properties and get rich. It's good entertainment but it's only for the professionals. If you're not in the Real Estate business full time and able to do most of the work yourself then it's not for you. The risk is too great and the profits too small. You don't need to spend money to learn how to loose money under the false impression that you will "Make a Fortune". Real Estate is the number one investment in America and you can ensure your future by building a secure investment real estate business.

You can also loose money by making bad decisions and in real estate you own the mistake when you own the property. The investment program that I outline in this book is conservative and very disciplined and is designed to avoid common mistakes and protect your investment. Nothing is perfect or guaranteed except Christ's love for you and the promises He's made to you. It's nice to know that there is truly something that is dependable, respectable, honorable and factual. Faith in yourself begins with having faith in something or someone that has stood the test of time. The advice in this book was inspired by Him and I am only the messenger. However, I made every mistake in real estate for 30 years so I am better able to appreciate and accept the truths contained in this book. I hope that you also have such faith in your life and that you have a belief system that is far beyond your own mortality.

Summary of our Disciplined Investment Plan:
1. Only buy New Single Family Homes
2. Only Buy in Growth Areas of the USA projecting 10% or more growth per year.
3. Don't pay over $100.00 per sq. ft.
4. Don't put more than 10 to 20% down payment.
5. Make sure it is a strong rental market with low unemployment
6. Before you close make sure the home is rent ready with the Salisbury Package.

Chapter 10

My Case Against the 1031 Exchange

It seems like we are becoming a country that depends more and more upon the Government to solve our problems even if the government is the source of those problems. Take, for example, the IRS collection of taxes on income, capital gains and estates. Although the tax rates and exemptions change for political exposition, they do not seem to go away. Although the tax rates change depending on whether the gain is short term or long term, most real estate investors deal with the latter. So, when an investor owns property for a period of time and the value of the property increases, they would like to trade it in for different property much like trading cars when the new models look so much better. The problem with selling is the creation of a tax obligation based upon the profits generated over the term of the investor's ownership. The gain may be greater based upon the length of time and the depreciation schedule used during ownership.

For example, you own this property for 10 years and purchased it originally for $105,000. and used a 27.5 year depreciation schedule. After ten years you have written off (depreciated) about $25,000 off the value of the improvement on the land (the house) and your cost basis is now $80,000. Since it is now worth $250,000. you will have taxes due on the $170,000. as long term capital gain. Your tax advisor suggests that you trade your property through a 1031 exchange and defer the taxes until some future date when you are in a lower tax bracket.

This tax deferral tool was introduced by the IRS on April 25, 1991 under regulation-Reg 1.1031(k)-1 and permits you to sell your property now and use the proceeds to purchase replacement property as long as you follow IRS rules, complete the purchase within a specified time period and use the services of a Qualified Intermediary who will insure that you exchange like kind investment property. Although the process is relatively safe if handled by a professional the potential for error is always present and you may end up buying a replacement property that is less than suitable in order to maintain your tax deferred status within the stated time period. The objective is clear and that is to avoid paying taxes now.

I have a better and more productive solution that is actually easier and not subject to the errors of a 1031 mistake. I advise my clients to refinance their appreciated property and use the net proceeds of the new loan to buy whatever they want whenever the right opportunity presents itself. No pressure, no IRS rules to deal with and less possibility of making an error.   Most important is the fact that you still own the original property and will continue to enjoy its further growth over the years. Since you did not sell, you do not have any tax to pay. You remain in control and can decide when to refinance and what you are going to buy with the net proceeds. You may choose to refinance to lower your interest rate, extend the maturity date or choose to just get a line of credit secured by your equity. That way you buy more property using the equity from the property that has appreciated. That's called using OPM and we don't need to explain that term to any real estate investors. You continue to depreciate the original property and add more property in order to build your real estate business. So why would you ever do a 1031 exchange? That is truly a fair question. As for me, I see no good reason to do it when you consider the simple option of refinancing and buying more of the best property in the best locations with no more than 10% down.

I can think of one 1031 exchange that makes some sense and that is to exchange vacant land for income producing property. The reason for my flexibility in this area is based upon the knowledge that you cannot borrow as much or as freely on vacant land as you can on income producing property. Deferring the capital gains on vacant land is also more attractive because your original cost is the basis for figuring your long term capital gains tax. You see, you cannot depreciate land only the improvements on the land. Also, you cannot leverage land in the same way you can leverage income producing property. Income property can be purchased with 10% down but raw land may take a 50% down payment because it is harder to finance. Sometime the seller will take back some paper but that usually has a shorter maturity date than a 30 year mortgage.

So, do a 1031 exchange to move from raw land to income producing property with my blessing. May all your gains be monumental but tax free.

Chapter 11

Go Zone IS A NO GO

Summary Report on the Go Zone Investment Proposal

The documentation provided in the attached report shows the pros and cons related to acquiring property in the area designated as the Go Zone (specific areas of interest have been highlighted in red). The majority of documentation found supports the "government's" position that this is an excellent opportunity for people wanting to invest in property in these areas. There is an overwhelming amount of information that supports their position.

After further research, it is apparent that there are significant problems associated with property located in the Go Zone. The majority of the problems found were documented in newspaper articles, television newscast videos and GAO reports.

There are problems with the rebuilding process especially with the infrastructure in the area. Business have moved out and jobs are harder to obtain. Depending on the specific county being reviewed, renovation has been seen at varying degrees—a few areas have rebuilt and are almost back on their feet while the majority of others have not made any or have made minimal progress.

New Orleans, Louisiana

Although New Orleans' situation is geographically magnificent, located at the mouth of the great Mississippi with its vast network of tributaries, the actual site is miserable, swampy land located in a dangerous, hostile environment, where the Mississippi debouches into the Gulf. The site's problems are numerous. The older and main parts of New Orleans rest on the natural levees of the Mississippi, about fifteen feet above sea level, with the firmest, most solid soil being silt. Most of the modern city is at or below sea level, with the Mississippi usually flowing past the city at a height of ten to fifteen feet above sea level, flooding at twenty feet.

Much of modern New Orleans is built on muck, with no solid bedrock until a depth of seventy feet is reached below the surface. Natural levees, which could be breached in floods, provided the only land access to the city, making land transportation tenuous at best.

The city is also open to hurricanes that periodically roar out of the Gulf, driving high tides ahead of them. The areas several feet above sea level are safe, but most of modern, especially suburban New Orleans is below sea level.

Finally, New Orleans is built on land that is gradually, in some cases even rapidly, sinking. http://www.madere.com/history.html

Mississippi, Alabama and Louisiana

The planning for the redevelopment of Mississippi and Alabama is making better progress than in Louisiana. In these two instances, the governors of these states knew how to work the system when it came to obtaining federal assistance. Both of these states contain flood plains where land was developed and homes built.

The redevelopment within these states has been encouraged by a massive influx of funds for use by private citizens and business owners. New building codes are being introduced, but always enforced. There is currently no moratorium on building in the flood plains again.

Summary

Overall, investing in property in the ravaged areas of Louisiana, Mississippi and Alabama is risky. The majority of the areas that were destroyed were either below sea level or in flood plains—making them susceptible to future hurricane and flooding damage.

The true question here is "how much are you willing to gamble?" The Gulf Coast has been hit by severe hurricanes throughout the years with moderate to severe damage occurring (depending on the strike zone). There can, and will, be other minor storms that hit the area that will cause flood damage—there will also, someday, be another Katrina.

Investing in distressed properties just because of a government created tax credit in the form of a one time 50% depreciation schedule is not good business unless the property is attractive without the tax benefits. The problems are many and are identified as follows:

1/ You buy the property you own it and you must determine what you're going to do with it. Ask simple questions like, is this good rental property? Are there good tenants available? Do they have jobs and is the local economy stable?

2/ Can you finance the property with 10% down? Can you even get insurance on the property considering that it is in a Go Zone for a purpose. What is the cost of the insurance and what will the lender require?

3/ Remember that the accelerated depreciation schedule which allowed you to recapture taxes from past years will result in greater capital gain should you decide to sell your property. For example, if you purchase a property for $150,000. and the value of the land is $50,000. then you can depreciate the improvement (home) from $100,000. down to $50,000. but if you sell the property for what you paid for it you will repay the government on the $50,000. profit.

The bottom line is this: The risk is too great and the rewards too little to spend any time finding property to buy in a "Go Zone". As a wrap I say..."Go Zone...Go Broke" or as they say in the game of Monopoly... **Pass** Go and **Keep** the $200.

Beware; Never buy any real estate because of some perceived Government Benefit.

Background Report

June 14, 2007

Positive Components /Aspects
Related to the
Go Zone

What is the GO Zone?

The Gulf Opportunity Zone Act (GO Zone) was signed into law by President Bush on Dec. 21, 2005. It established tax incentives and bond provisions to support the rebuilding of and capital investments in local and regional economies in parts of Louisiana, Mississippi and Alabama that were devastated by the hurricanes in 2005. The GO Zone encompasses more than 20 parishes in Louisiana, approximately 50 counties in Mississippi and 11 counties in western and southern Alabama.

The GO Zone legislation allows private business owners and corporations to borrow capital through tax-exempt financing to acquire, construct, reconstruct or renovate nonresidential real property, qualified residential rental projects, and public utility property in the affected areas. Tax-exempt borrowing provides lower cost of capital than conventional debt financing. Alternatively, the borrowers have the opportunity to take accelerated depreciation in the first year equal to 50% of the cost of new capital investments.

GO Zone bonds must meet certain guidelines, including:
- Must be located within the Zone.
- 95% or more of net proceeds are used for "qualified project costs".
- Projects must be approved by the Governor of the State.
- Bonds must be issued by Dec. 31, 2010.
- Election for depreciation benefit expires at end of the 2008 calendar year.

What types of business are eligible for this financing?

Tax-exempt financing has been largely limited to governmental agencies or not-for-profit organizations. However, under the GO Zone Act, a wide range of businesses, including public and private corporations, retailers, commercial developers, utilities and hospitals, have the opportunity to build or rebuild at interest rates that can be as much as 1.5% to 2% below conventional financing options. http://www.gozonebonds.com/

Under present law, a taxpayer is allowed to recover, through annual depreciation deductions, the cost of certain property used in a trade or business or for the production of income. The amount of the depreciation deduction allowed with respect to tangible property for a taxable year is determined under the modified accelerated cost recovery system (MACRS). Most new business equipment can be either depreciated over its class life or expensed immediately under Internal Revenue Code Section 179. Under the GO Zone Act, taxpayers are now allowed an additional depreciation deduction equal to 50% of the depreciable basis of qualified Gulf Opportunity Zone property for the first year the property is placed in service. New GO Zone property cannot qualify for both tax-exempt bond financing and the 50% bonus depreciation. http://www.gozoneguide.com/story_4.html

Guide to Redevelopment

This is the most aggressive set of business incentives in U.S. history, and will drive economic restoration and rebuilding of Louisiana communities impacted by hurricanes Katrina and Rita.

This guide will illustrate the key financial incentives included in the Gulf Opportunity Zone legislation. Gulf Opportunity Zone provisions such as 50 percent bonus depreciation of capital costs or $7.9 billion in tax-exempt private activity bonds offer outstanding investment opportunities to both large and small businesses. Combine these federal programs with our portfolio of existing federal and state incentives, and you'll see that Louisiana is an extremely attractive destination for business location and expansion. http://www.gozoneguide.com/letter.html

Louisiana GO Zone Private Activity Bonds

The Gulf Zone Opportunity Zone Act will provide private businesses and corporations in Louisiana with the opportunity to finance construction and reconstruction of projects through the issuance of tax-exempt bonds. The Act provides for approximately $7.9 billion in additional authority for Louisiana and its political subdivisions to issue private activity bonds. Private business owners and corporations may borrow tax-exempt money to cover the costs of acquiring, constructing and renovating nonresidential real property located in the GO Zone. Issuance of any bonds authorized under this provision must also be approved by Governor Blanco.

Louisiana Parishes in the GO Zone

Acadia, Ascension, Assumption, Calcasieu, Cameron, East Baton Rouge, East Feliciana, Iberia, Iberville, Jefferson, Jefferson Davis, Lafayette, Lafourche, Livingston, Orleans, Pointe Coupee, Plaquemines, St. Bernard, St. Charles, St. Helena, St. James, St. John the Baptist, St. Mary, St. Martin, St. Tammany, Tangipahoa, Terrebonne, Vermillion, Washington, West Baton Rouge, and West Feliciana. (Parishes shown in orange on this **map**):

http://www.gozonebonds.com/pdfs/LA_GO_Zone_FEMA_Map.pdf

Projects That Qualify for Tax-exempt Financing

Eligible projects may include, *but are not limited to*: retail stores, warehouses, manufacturing facilities, industrial plants, office buildings, bank branches, hotels and motels, restaurants, physician office buildings, medical hospitals and clinics.

The Benefits of GO Zone Bond Project Financing

Interest on bonds is exempt from federal and State of Louisiana income taxes; therefore the interest rate is lower than through conventional financing, historically saving a borrower 1.50% to 2.00%. Congress has also excluded the interest on the GOZB from Alternative Minimum Taxation.

Special Depreciation Election Benefit

The Act permits businesses to claim an additional first year depreciation deduction equal to 50 % of the cost of new capital investments made in the Zone (depreciation will be taken in lieu of tax-exempt financing). The depreciation deduction is exempt from AMT, does not require approval by the State, and applies to property placed in service prior to January 1, 2008, or January 1, 2009 for real property. We recommend consultation with your certified public accountant regarding qualification and treatment of this benefit. Morgan Keegan and Regions welcome the opportunity to assist in evaluating and executing taxable or conventional financing alternatives for those who select the depreciation deduction.

Advance Refunding Benefit for Municipal Debt

The Act provides for an approximate $4.5 billion of funds to permit an additional advance refunding opportunity for municipal debt. Through this, the State, parishes, municipalities, etc. may apply to the Governor's office for an allocation of the proceeds. This opportunity is NOT restricted solely to the Zone; it applies to ALL Louisiana parishes. http://www.gozonebonds.com/louisiana.html

Go Zone Maps

Alabama Go Zone Info   Louisiana Go Zone Info   Mississippi Go Zone Info

http://www.gozone-info.com/maps.cfm

Alabama Go Zone:
http://www.gozone-info.com/state_gozone_al.cfm

Louisiana Go Zone:
http://www.gozone-info.com/state_gozone_la.cfm

Mississippi Go Zone:
http://www.gozone-info.com/state_gozone_ms.cfm

Enhancement of Low Income Housing Tax Credits

2005 (H.R. 4440) includes several provisions important to real estate. The GO Zone Act provides for a greater allocation of low-income housing tax credits for the affected areas, increases the number of persons that qualify as low-income, and increases the amount of financing that results from using the credit. These liberalizations make building in the GO Zone more attractive to investors both in terms of the amount of the credit available and the threshold for poverty that tenants must meet.

http://www.gozoneonline.com/

Alabama GO Zone Private Activity Bonds

The Gulf Zone Opportunity Zone Act will provide private businesses and corporations in Alabama with the opportunity to finance construction and reconstruction of projects through the issuance of tax-exempt bonds.

The Act provides for approximately $2.1 billion in additional authority for Alabama and its political subdivisions to issue private activity bonds. Private business owners and corporations may borrow tax-exempt money to cover the costs of acquiring, constructing and renovating nonresidential real property located in the GO Zone. Issuance of any bonds authorized under this provision must also be approved by Governor Riley.

Alabama Counties in the GO Zone

Tuscaloosa, Pickens, Sumter, Greene, Hale, Marengo, Choctaw, Clarke, Washington, Mobile and Baldwin counties. (Counties shown in orange on this **map**):

http://www.gozonebonds.com/pdfs/AL_GO_Zone_FEMA_Map.pdf

Projects That Qualify for Tax-exempt Financing

Eligible projects may include, *but are not limited to*: retail stores, warehouses, manufacturing facilities, industrial plants, office buildings, bank branches, hotels and motels, restaurants, physician office buildings, medical hospitals and clinics.

The Benefits of GO Zone Bond Project Financing

Interest on bonds is exempt from federal and State of Alabama income taxes; therefore the interest rate is lower than through conventional financing, historically saving a borrower 1.50% to 2.00%. Congress has also excluded the interest on the GOZB from Alternative Minimum Taxation.

Special Depreciation Election Benefit

The Act permits businesses to claim an additional first year depreciation deduction equal to 50 % of the cost of new capital investments made in the Zone (depreciation will be taken in lieu of tax-exempt financing). The depreciation deduction is exempt from AMT, does not require approval by the State, and applies to property placed in service prior to January 1, 2008, or January 1, 2009 for real property. We recommend consultation with your certified public accountant regarding qualification and treatment of this benefit. Morgan Keegan and Regions welcome the opportunity to assist in evaluating and executing taxable or conventional financing alternatives for those who select the depreciation deduction.

Advance Refunding Benefit for Municipal Debt

The Act provides for an approximate $1.125 billion of funds to permit an additional advance refunding opportunity for municipal debt. Through this, the State, counties, municipalities, etc. may apply to the Governor's office for an allocation of the proceeds. This opportunity is NOT restricted solely to the Zone; it applies to ALL Alabama counties. http://www.gozonebonds.com/alabama.html

Mississippi GO Zone Private Activity Bonds

The Gulf Zone Opportunity Zone Act will provide private businesses and corporations in Mississippi with the opportunity to finance construction and reconstruction of projects through the issuance of tax-exempt bonds.

The Act provides for approximately $4.8 billion in additional authority for Mississippi and its political subdivisions to issue private activity bonds. Private business owners and corporations may borrow tax-exempt money to cover the costs of acquiring, constructing and renovating nonresidential real property located in the GO Zone.

Issuance of any bonds authorized under this provision must also be approved by Governor Barbour.

Mississippi Counties in the GO Zone

Adams, Amite, Attala, Claiborne, Choctaw, Clarke, Copiah, Covington, Forrest, Franklin, George, Greene, Hancock, Harrison, Hinds, Holmes, Humphreys, Jackson, Jasper, Jefferson, Jefferson Davis, Jones, Kemper, Lamar, Lauderdale, Lawrence, Leake, Lincoln, Lowndes, Madison, Marion, Neshoba, Newton, Noxubee, Oktibbeha, Pearl River, Perry, Pike, Rankin, Scott, Simpson, Smith, Stone, Walthall, Warren, Wayne, Wilkinson, Winston and Yazoo (Counties shown in orange on this **map**)
http://www.gozonebonds.com/pdfs/MS_GO_Zone_FEMA_Map.pdf

Projects That Qualify for Tax-exempt Financing

Eligible projects may include, *but are not limited to*: retail stores, warehouses, manufacturing facilities, industrial plants, office buildings, bank branches, hotels and motels, restaurants, physician office buildings, medical hospitals and clinics.

The Benefits of GO Zone Bond Project Financing

Interest on bonds is exempt from federal and State of Mississippi income taxes; therefore the interest rate is lower than through conventional financing, historically saving a borrower 1.50% to 2.00%. Congress has also excluded the interest on the GOZB from Alternative Minimum Taxation.

Special Depreciation Election Benefit

The Act permits businesses to claim an additional first year depreciation deduction equal to 50 % of the cost of new capital investments made in the Zone (depreciation will be taken in lieu of tax-exempt financing). The depreciation deduction is exempt from AMT, does not require approval by the State, and applies to property placed in service prior to January 1, 2008, or January 1, 2009 for real property. We recommend consultation with your certified public accountant regarding qualification and treatment of this benefit. Morgan Keegan and Regions welcome the opportunity to assist in evaluating and executing taxable or conventional financing alternatives for those who select the depreciation deduction.

Advance Refunding Benefit for Municipal Debt

The Act provides for an approximate $2.25 billion of funds to permit an additional advance refunding opportunity for municipal debt. Through this, the State, counties, municipalities, etc. may apply to the Governor's office for an allocation of the proceeds. This opportunity is NOT restricted solely to the Zone; it applies to ALL Mississippi counties.

http://www.gozonebonds.com/mississippi.html

Background Report

June 14, 2007

Negative Components/Aspects

Related to the
Go Zone

The GO Zone Won't Go: Lessons for Gulf Opportunity Zones
By John Alexander Burton
November 9, 2005

Read the full report (PDF): http://www.americanprogress.org/kf/GO_ZONE.PDF

EXECUTIVE SUMMARY On September 15, 2005, two weeks after Hurricane Katrina's landfall on the Gulf Coast, President Bush proposed a new Gulf Opportunity Zone (GO Zone) to rebuild the economy of the devastated region. The President had first proposed the Opportunity Zones a year earlier, when he addressed the 2004 Republican Convention. These zones would offer lower tax rates, investment incentives and regulatory relief. This proposal can be compared to earlier efforts at job creation in underdeveloped areas. In 1993, President Clinton's first "round" of Empowerment Zones (EZ) and Enterprise Communities (EC) combined flexible block grants for locally-determined services with tax incentives to encourage investment and hiring. Conservatives in Congress expanded the tax incentives while restricting the promised grants funding to the later rounds of EZ/ECs. Also, the Renewal Community (RC) initiative, championed by conservatives, offers tax breaks in the place of direct grants. The successes and failures of the EZ/EC/RC initiatives can inform an analysis of the proposed "GO Zone." The chief conclusions of this report are that:

> **TAX INCENTIVES FOR RENEWAL COMMUNITIES ARE NOT COST-EFFICIENT:** The RC wage credit created jobs for RC residents at an average cost of $34,911 (2004 dollars) and the commercial revitalization deduction created new jobs at an average cost of $85,853 (2004 dollars). Round I and Round II EZ workforce development programs generated jobs for EZ residents at an average cost of $2,831 (2004 dollars) and $5,315 (2004 dollars) respectively. Compared to the EZ workforce development programs, the RC tax incentives create jobs for RC residents at a higher cost to the federal government (Figure 1). Nonetheless, RC tax incentives like the commercial

revitalization deduction (CRD) and the wage credit receive larger federal expenditures than the more cost-efficient EZ workforce development programs receive (Figure 2).

FUNDED EZ/EC PROGRAMS CREATED JOBS: The EZ/EC economic opportunity programs have generated over 290,000 job opportunities for EZ/EC residents.

TAX INCENTIVES FOR RENEWAL COMMUNITIES ARE NOT WIDELY USED: Despite the RC marketing efforts and outreach to businesses, the average take-up rates for the RC tax incentives range from 0 percent to 4 percent.

TAX INCENTIVES ALONE HAVE LIMITED VALUE: Many individuals and businesses in distressed communities have little if any federal tax liability. EZ administrators indicate that these tax incentives were not particularly helpful in stimulating new investment.

THERE IS A HIGH RISK OF TAX FRAUD: GAO reports indicate that the IRS does not collect the data necessary to verify that EZ/EC/RC tax incentives are not claimed by ineligible or out-of area tax filers. Nor is the IRS tracking tax benefit amounts in the New York Liberty Zone. These tax policies present high risks for the Gulf Region. http://www.americanprogress.org/issues/2005/11/b1170683.html

U.S. Army Corps of Engineers' Procurement of Pumping Systems for the New Orleans Drainage Canals GAO-07-908R
http://www.gao.gov/new.items/d07908r.pdfMay 23, 2007 PDF
http://www.gao.gov/new.items/d07908r.pdf
Accessible Text http://www.gao.gov/htext/d07908r.html

To avoid flooding in New Orleans after a rain storm, the city's Sewerage and Water Board pumps rainwater from the city into three drainage canals which then flow unrestricted into Lake Pontchartrain. While critical to prevent flooding from rainfall, these canals are vulnerable to storm surge from Lake Pontchartrain during a hurricane, and consequently are lined with floodwalls along both sides to protect storm surge from overtopping the canals and flooding the city. However, during Hurricane Katrina, several breaches occurred in the canal floodwalls allowing significant amounts of water to enter New Orleans from Lake Pontchartrain. In its efforts to restore pre-Katrina levels of hurricane protection to New Orleans by the June 1st start of the 2006 hurricane season, in late 2005, the U.S. Army Corps of Engineers (Corps) considered strengthening the drainage canal floodwalls but decided to postpone this effort due to cost and time constraints. Instead, the Corps decided to install three interim closure structures (gates) at the points where the canals meet the lake. These gates would be closed during major storm events to prevent storm surge from entering the canals and potentially breaching the canal floodwalls and flooding the city. Due to space constraints along the canals and the limited amount of time it had before the start of the 2006 hurricane season, the Corps decided to procure 34 large-capacity hydraulic pumping systems1 to provide the most pumping capacity possible by June 1, 2006. The Corps acknowledged that its decision to install the gates and provide pumping capacity that was less than what was needed to keep the city dry could result in some flooding by rainfall but believed that the risk from a hurricane-induced storm surge was far greater than the risk of flooding from heavy rainfall. During the process of acquiring, testing, and installing the pumping systems for the drainage canals, many concerns were raised by the media about potential problems with the operation of these pumping systems, and GAO was asked to examine the

(1) specifications and requirements of the contract and the basis for selecting the supplier of the pumping systems; (2) concerns identified during factory testing and the Corps' rationale to install the pumping systems in light of the factory test failures; (3) actions the Corps has taken to address the known problems with the pumping systems; and (4) pumping capacity that existed on June 1, 2006, the capacity that currently exists, and the capacity that is planned for the 2007 hurricane season.

The Corps' decisions to acquire the 34 hydraulic pumping systems were focused on satisfying its commitment to have pumping capacity on the drainage canals in place by June 1, 2006--the start of the 2006 hurricane season. In order to increase the likelihood that pumping capacity would be in place when needed, the Corps utilized several tools to expedite and streamline the acquisition process. The Corps appears to have had a valid reason for each of the iterative decisions it made at each stage of the procurement process. Factory testing of the pumps occurred from March through May 2006, and revealed several problems with specific components of the pumping systems. As a result of the concerns identified during factory testing, the Corps had no assurance that the pumping systems would operate to capacity when needed. Nevertheless, the pumping systems were installed as planned because the Corps believed that it was better to have some pumping capacity along the drainage canals during the 2006 hurricane season rather than none. Since June 1, 2006, the Corps has continued to take steps to correct known performance problems with the pumping systems, including uninstalling them to make some repairs. On June 1, 2006, the Corps had installed 11 pumping systems, and by July 2006, it had installed 34, although it is uncertain how much of the theoretical capacity of these pumping systems would have worked and for how long. By June 1, 2007, the Corps plans to complete the reinstallation of all 40 pumping systems that have been repaired and each has been tested for between 45 minutes to 2 hours, thus providing greater assurance that they will perform as designed during the upcoming 2007 hurricane season. However, the total planned pumping capacity will still not meet the Sewerage and Water Board's drainage needs to keep the city from flooding during a hurricane when the canal gates are closed.

http://www.gao.gov/docdblite/summary.php?rptno=GAO-07908R&accno=A69986

Television web site – Video leads – WDSU.com
Evacuating The Louisiana Coast
(http://www.wdsu.com/video/13414915/index.html)
Learn more about how officials plan to have residents evacuate the Louisiana coast.

St. Bernard Leaders Say They're More Prepared
http://www.wdsu.com/video/13415973/index.html

St. Tammany Emergency HQ Gets Revamped
http://www.wdsu.com/video/13415755/index.html
J.P. Schools Plan Post-Hurricane Response
http://www.wdsu.com/video/13414961/index.html

Parish Placards Needed To Re-Enter After Storm
http://www.wdsu.com/video/13347145/index.html

6 Changes In 6 Parishes
http://www.wdsu.com/video/13414901/index.html

The Safest Places: St. Tammany Parish
http://www.wdsu.com/video/13348648/index.html

St. Tammany Parish Neighborhood At Risk
http://www.wdsu.com/video/13350752/index.html

The Safest Places: Orleans Parish
http://www.wdsu.com/video/13339614/index.html

The Neighborhood Most At Risk In Orleans Parish
http://www.wdsu.com/video/13343168/index.html

The Safest Places To Live In Jefferson Parish
http://www.wdsu.com/video/13330348/index.html

NWS Official Talks About Storm Surge
http://www.wdsu.com/video/11536222/index.html

Gray's Colleague Talks About Hurricane Predictions
http://www.wdsu.com/video/11536725/index.html
http://www.wdsu.com/hurricanes/index.html

Publication--Institute for Southern Studies— Facing South

June 3, 2007, 11:27AM -- Mississippi communities hope to avoid sprawl in rebuild

OCEAN SPRINGS, Miss. — A few weeks after Hurricane Katrina swept away Marty Wagoner's beachfront home and guest cottage, the swamp behind his property offered up an unexpected gift. Mucking around in the knee-deep water one day, Wagoner found big chunks of the oak floors from his house. He salvaged the wood, dried it out and installed it in his new cottage, where it gleams with the promise of lives resumed if not fully reclaimed.

Wagoner, a financial consultant, didn't hesitate for a moment about whether to rebuild on a little hill overlooking the unprotected beach. "This is paradise here," he said, looking out at the morning sun glinting off Biloxi Bay.

Twenty-one months after Katrina, as the devastated Mississippi Gulf Coast staggers to its feet, Wagoner is among thousands of home and business owners whose choices will determine what this 70-mile stretch of coastline looks like after hundreds of millions of dollars in federal reconstruction funds are spent.

Wagoner's new cottage and the larger house that will soon rise next to it were designed by Bruce Tolar, an Ocean Springs architect who is leading an effort to ensure that neighborhoods leveled by Katrina retain their walkable, small-town form when they are rebuilt.

Most of Mississippi's coastal communities, with the notable exception of Biloxi, are embracing the SmartCode, a planning system that encourages neighborhoods with homes, businesses and civic buildings clustered close to one another.

They hope this approach will prevent the impending redevelopment from being dominated by high-rise condos and hulking casinos interspersed with T-shirt shops, strip centers and big-box stores surrounded by vast parking lots. Opportunities for this kind of development are abundant along U.S. 90, which remains mostly a wasteland of empty slabs and front porch steps that lead to nothing.

The concerns drift farther inland, where thousands of homes and businesses in older, low-lying neighborhoods surrounding back bays were washed away by Katrina's record-breaking storm surge, which was higher than 30 feet in some places. In many cases, updated zoning codes would prohibit them from being rebuilt in their original form.

"We're creating our coastal history in building a community today,"

Tolar said. "You can't go back and take that day back. You say, 'What can we do to make it better? What do we value about this place?' "

Residents of Galveston and other coastal cities could find themselves asking the same questions if they were struck by a storm as vicious as Katrina, said Ricky Mathews, the publisher of the Sun-Herald newspaper and a member of Gov.

Haley Barbour's Commission on Recovery, Rebuilding and Renewal.

"If Katrina had hit Galveston, it wouldn't exist," said Mathews, who joined a delegation of Mississippi leaders on a visit to Galveston in March 2006. "It would have annihilated the entire island."

The enthusiasm for the SmartCode extends to the grass roots — to people like Sister Martha Milner of Mercy Housing and Human Development in Pass Christian, which lost about 2,500 of its 3,000 homes to Katrina.

Standing on a narrow street in the center of town, Milner pointed out a church and a brick building that could house a community center. Across the street, a new cottage stood surrounded by empty lots and an abandoned, crumbling shack.

"Our thought was to build back a sense of neighborhood and community," Milner said. "We want to put in sidewalks and make this a walkable neighborhood."

Pass Christian's recovery is barely past the cleanup stage. The city government and police and fire departments still operate in temporary buildings, and the tax base remains so minimal that coming up with the small local match required for certain federal reconstruction grants has been difficult.

Around town, though, the streets are dotted with the skeletal beginnings of new houses, mostly being built by volunteers from faith-based nonprofits from as far away as Michigan and Canada.

Arthur Conway, 64, known to his friends and family as Ootie, hopes to move into his house in the next month or so. His longtime employers, grateful for his years of service and his help in caring for an aging relative, helped build it.

"The people I work for, they said, I did for their mother and it was time for them to do for me," Conway said as he showed off his nearly complete new house. "It was one of the best feelings in my life."

A friend, local contractor Jim Schmitt, said volunteers sometimes had an ulterior motive when they showed up to help.

"Ootie makes the best gumbo and ribs in town," Schmitt said, smiling at his friend. "I'd come here and pretend to work just to eat."

Many new homes in Pass Christian are small cottages that were assembled elsewhere and shipped in. Schmitt, a New Orleans native who has lived in the community for more than 30 years, worries that these prefabricated houses will deteriorate in a few years while the neighborhoods surrounding them decay into slums.

"They're a step above trailers, but they're not what they're purported to be," he said. "Just because someone is poor doesn't mean you have to give them something minimal. I think we as a community can do better."

Anthony Hall, an alderman in Pass Christian, has a different view. He said the prebuilt cottages provide desperately needed affordable homes that are gradually restoring the town's tax base.

Mississippi's coastal communities certainly are still struggling economically, in part because of a significant loss of population. New subdivisions are springing up north of Interstate 10, and some builders expect a permanent population shift away from the coast.

The state's three coastal counties suffered a net loss of more than 32,000 residents between July 2005, the month before Katrina, and July 2006, census figures show. The three counties to the north gained about 6,000 people.

Katrina wiped out important local industries, such as oystering, which are just beginning to recover.

Under such conditions, a certain tension can develop between the economic and psychological benefits of rebuilding quickly and the long-term importance of rebuilding well.

For example, Schmitt said, building codes were tightened after Katrina, and new homes must be elevated much higher — as high as 16 feet above ground level in some places compared with 7 feet before the hurricane. But local officials sometimes are reluctant to enforce these rules too rigorously because they don't want to be seen as holding up recovery, he said.

Hall said the elevation requirements add to construction costs and create a serious problem for elderly residents who have difficulty climbing so many steps. Federal officials are insisting on the higher elevations as a condition of obtaining flood insurance.

"How do you fight the government?" Hall asked.

Hall and his colleagues on Pass Christian's Board of Aldermen recently voted to adopt the text of the SmartCode as a guide for their community's recovery. The town, like Gulfport and others along the coast, is working on the maps and neighborhood plans necessary to use the code effectively.

Biloxi, however, is taking a different path. The coast's second-largest city after Gulfport, with a population of about 50,000, was not convinced by the architects and planners who came to the area a month after Katrina and organized SmartCode planning sessions, said Jerry Creel, Biloxi's director of community development.

Biloxi has hired a private firm to develop a new master plan and land-development ordinance, and that plan might include some elements of the SmartCode, Creel said.

SmartCode supporters acknowledge that no planning tool is a panacea for an area that has undergone such an immense tragedy. The usual post-disaster problems — crooked contractors, scarce materials, land speculation, political infighting — have cropped up here, limiting the time and energy available for planning.

But in recent months, with the cleanup largely complete and a bit of time to take a breath, south Mississippians have been taking stock of what's important to them and plotting strategies to hang onto it.

"No one lives in this town because they're getting rich," said Schmitt, relaxing with a cold drink on the porch of his renovated home, which was flooded by Katrina. "They're here for the quality of life."

Some residents, unable to muster the will or resources to rebuild, are clinging to tiny remnants of that life.

Along U.S. 90 in Long Beach, just east of Pass Christian, two small, stooped figures walked slowly around a bare foundation slab one recent morning. Henry Occhi, 88, and his wife Rita, 87, were picking blackberries from a bush on the property where their home stood before Katrina.

The couple built the house for their retirement 10 years ago.

They wanted to rebuild, but the cost of insurance, which in creased dramatically after Katrina, was a daunting obstacle. Rita Occhi said it's likely the couple will remain in their rented house in a nearby town.

"It's too late for us to build back," she said, opening her hand to display a few fat, glistening berries. "But I loved it." http://www.chron.com/disp/story.mpl/headline/nation/4857397.ht ml
April 10, 2006, 1:55PM

Vulnerable coast faces new storm season

By MICHAEL KUNZELMAN

Associated Press

GULFPORT, Miss. — Joe Spraggins knows it will take stockpiles of food, water and fuel and better evacuation routes to survive if the Gulf Coast gets hit by another monster storm this coming hurricane season.

What the Harrison County emergency management director cannot fully plan for is the psychological toll another hurricane could exact on residents struggling to rebuild their lives after Katrina.

"They're already at the point of breaking," he said. "If we have another storm of any size this summer, mental health is going to be a huge issue."

Katrina laid waste to tens of thousands of homes and businesses and killed more than 1,300 people in Louisiana and Mississippi. Now, less than two months before the next hurricane season starts June 1, overworked officials and frazzled homeowners are bracing for the possibility of another killer storm in a region where thousands still live in government-issued trailers or under blue tarps.

This hurricane season could be more brutal than last year's, when a record-setting 27 storms, including 15 hurricanes, churned in the Atlantic Ocean. Forecasters say the Atlantic is in a period of increased hurricane activity that could last another a decade or longer.

Even a weaker storm than Katrina could be devastating, wiping out much of the modest progress that has been made and sweeping away the little trailers.

Mississippi Gov. Haley Barbour calls this a "critical period of vulnerability."

"We're going to pray for the best but prepare for the worst," he said.

Spraggins, whose territory includes Katrina-battered Gulfport and Biloxi, said the county is devising a new emergency plan to replace the old one.

Katrina made a mockery out of federal, state and local emergency plans. Evacuation routes were clogged, communications were spotty, and emergency supplies were not positioned to arrive quickly in the areas of greatest need.

"We will never be prepared to take a Katrina, but we will be prepared to do a lot better than we did the last time," Spraggins said.

In Mississippi, about 99,000 people are living in more than 36,000 FEMA trailers and mobile homes. In Louisiana, more than 51,000 trailers dot the landscape.

Many people whose homes were demolished by Katrina also lost cars and trucks, meaning it could be difficult for them to get out if another storm threatens. As a result, evacuations will start earlier and will be conducted more often, Barbour warned.

"We're going to have to decide earlier to evacuate because it's going to take longer," Barbour said. "And also, because of the flimsiness of the travel trailers, we will probably evacuate sometimes when we didn't really need to. But we can't take the risk because the travel trailers are extremely vulnerable."

Likewise, the coast's natural defenses have never been weaker. Katrina, followed by Hurricane Rita a month later, ripped apart a band of barrier islands and wetlands that help soften a hurricane's blow.

"These barrier islands are in many places the first line of defense for the mainland," said Abby Sallenger, an oceanographer for the U.S. Geological Survey. "If we have another hurricane hit, how much worse will the impact be?"

Katrina also left the region's economy in tatters, especially in New Orleans.

A report issued in February by Louisiana-based economist Loren Scott found that metropolitan New Orleans' employment rate remained 32 percent below its pre-Katrina peak, or down 198,000 jobs. Scott worries that a lot of employers will give up if another destructive storm hits New Orleans.

"All of these companies are willing to be part of the 'Save New Orleans' movement once," he said. "I just wonder if they're willing to be part of it twice."

Katrina dealt a crippling blow to southern Mississippi's economy, as well, but its casino industry is recovering and the scenic 70-mile coastline has condominium developers salivating.

"People still want to have their home or condominium look out on the water, and that's going to remain a serious draw," Scott said.

Katrina destroyed Daniel's South Beach Restaurant and Bar, a beachfront watering hole in Bay St. Louis that Ray Murphy's family has operated for more than 25 years. Murphy is about to reopen the restaurant in an old Knights of Columbus hall, about a half-mile from the beach.

Murphy said the threat of another destructive hurricane never factored into his decision to rebuild.

"One of these days, I'm going to give it up — but not yet," he said. "I'm not ready to throw in the towel."

Neither is Scott Oliver, a longtime Gulfport resident. On a cement slab with a clear view of the beach, he is building a storm-resistent "fort" to replace the quaint wood-frame house that Katrina blasted into splinters and shards.

Oliver poured the first two concrete walls — 12 feet high and 12 inches thick — in early March, copying features of buildings that survived Katrina.

"I had a structural engineer tell me the first floor would qualify as a tornado shelter," boasted Oliver, 59, a project manager for a building contractor.

Oliver started drawing the blueprints less than a week after Katrina. But first he had to convince his wife, Caprice, that rebuilding so close to the coast is not foolish or reckless. The thought of losing everything — again — is almost unbearable.

Said his wife: "I don't necessarily believe that's the last Katrina we're going to see."

http://www.chron.com/disp/story.mpl/special/05/katrina/3784004.html

Friday, June 01, 2007

Reuters picks up on Mississippi recovery story

(http://southernstudies.org/facingsouth/2007/06/reuters-picks-upon-mississippi.asp)

Following our coverage in Salon last week (http://www.salon.com/news/feature/2007/05/25/mississippi/index.html) about the slow pace of recovery in **post-Katrina Mississippi** -- "slower than molasses in winter," one resident told us --Reuters has a piece (http://news.yahoo.com/s/nm/20070531/us_nm/katrina_towns_ge neral_feature_pict_dc) on small towns struggling to rebuild in the Magnolia State.

Like our piece, the story looks at **Pearlington**, the small town 40 minutes up from New Orleans that was "ground zero" for Katrina. Reuters describes a scene similar to what we found: The local school and post office remain closed, few businesses have reopened and only a quarter of its 800 homes have been rebuilt, according to Glenn Locklin of the charity One House at a Time.

"You don't hear about us anymore. They say we're not news," Locklin said. "The one thing people don't realize is that we are just as bad as we were."

The devastation in coastal Mississippi is all the more shocking given the disproportionate share of federal relief dollars (http://www.salon.com/news/feature/2007/05/25/mississippi/index .html) **Gov. Haley Barbour** was able to attract for his state. For example, even though Louisiana suffered 75% of the housing damage from Katrina, Mississippi raked in 70% of **FEMA**'s money for the Alternative Housing Pilot Program. Similar disparities can be found on funding from health care to schools.

Friday, May 25, 2007

Gulf Watch: Our story in Salon investigates Barbour's "Mississippi Miracle"

(http://southernstudies.org/facingsouth/2007/05/our-story-insalon-investigates.asp)

Since Katrina, Mississippi Gov. Haley Barbour has received heaps of praise for his political savvy and ability to use his GOP connections to get a lion's share of federal relief funds for his state.

But with all the honors and money, how is the Mississippi recovery going? My colleague Sue Sturgis and I investigate in a special report published at Salon today. (http://www.salon.com/news/feature/2007/05/25/mississippi/)

One eye-opening item we found is just how lopsided Mississippi's take of Katrina relief has been: Consider the Gulf Coast housing crisis, one of the key issues that has kept nearly half the population of New Orleans from returning to the city since Katrina. More than **75 percent of the housing damage from the storm was in Louisiana, but Mississippi has received 70 percent of the funds through FEMA's Alternative Housing Pilot Program.** Of the $388 million available, FEMA gave a Mississippi program offering upgraded trailers more than $275 million. Meanwhile, the agency awarded Louisiana's "Katrina Cottage" program, which features more permanent modular homes for storm victims, a mere $75 million.

It's not just housing. Mississippi is also slated to get 38 percent of federal hospital recovery funds, even though it lost just 79 beds compared to 2,600 lost in southern Louisiana, which will get 45 percent of the funds. Mississippi and Louisiana both received $95 million to offset losses in higher education, even though Louisiana was home to 75 percent of displaced students. The states also received $100 million each for K-12 students affected by the storms, despite the fact that 69 percent resided in Louisiana. Barbour insists that Congress is "getting its money's worth" for all it's given to Mississippi -- but how is the state's recovery really going?

For the residents of Hancock County, Barbour and Mississippi's ability to capture the lion's share of Katrina relief dollars makes the slow progress in their area all the more demoralizing. The county's 911 system still operates out of a trailer. Damaged wastewater and drainage systems frustrate hopes of a return to normalcy; earlier this month in Waveland, 16 miles east of Pearlington, a 9-and-a-half-foot alligator was found swimming in a drainage ditch next to a bus stop at 8 o'clock in the morning. Mayor Tommy Longo says the creatures freely roam throughout devastated residential areas.

As we point out, even worse is the fact that Barbour won't use Mississippi's recent tax windfall to help devastated coastal communities that are drowning in $79 million of debt. It's so bad, some towns are afraid they'll go bankrupt entirely:

"One thing you continually hear from officials from FEMA to the state level is that -- and they love this phrase -they've 'never seen a city go under because of a natural disaster,'" [Waveland mayor] Longo says. "But there have been so many firsts in Katrina."

Thursday, May 17, 2007

Gulf Watch: Problems still beset hurricane readiness systems

(http://southernstudies.org/facingsouth/2007/05/problems-stillbeset-hurricane.asp)

With what's expected to be an unusually active (http://tropical.atmos.colostate.edu/Forecasts/) hurricane season just weeks away, concern is mounting about serious problems still afflicting the nation's readiness and response systems almost two years after Hurricane Katrina.

This week the new director of the National Hurricane Center (http://www.nhc.noaa.gov/) charged that his superiors are wasting millions of dollars on unnecessary public-relations efforts while shortchanging storm forecasters, the Miami Herald reported (http://www.nhc.noaa.gov/): Bill Proenza, who took the hurricane center post in January, said top officials at the National Oceanic and Atmospheric Administration are spending $4 million on a ''bogus'' 200year NOAA anniversary celebration.

That celebration is part of a broader campaign to publicize NOAA and its leaders, Proenza and other critics said, while diminishing the identity of its best-known components, the National Weather Service and the hurricane center.

Meanwhile, Proenza said, NOAA has cut $700,000 from a crucial hurricane research program and allowed other important initiatives to go unfunded, but it wants to spend money to change the widely recognized center's name to the "NOAA Hurricane Center."

In the immediate aftermath of Hurricane Katrina, Proenza and former hurricane center director Max Mayfield said, NOAA even ordered them to remove the National Weather Service logo from official tracking maps and retain only the NOAA logo. They refused. Proenza told the paper that it's getting to the point that he "cannot tolerate" the situation.

FEMA Director R. David Paulison also raised concerns about NOAA's re-branding effort, urging the agency to "not make a rash decision," the paper reported. The fear is that if the National Weather Service (http://www.nws.noaa.gov/) loses its identity, its funding would be absorbed -- and possibly diluted -- by NOAA.

Proenza and Paulison made their comments during press interviews while attending the Florida Governor's Hurricane Conference (http://www.flghc.org/) taking place this week at the Broward County Convention Center. Meanwhile, Paulison on Tuesday admitted during a House Homeland Security hearing -- titled "The 2007 Hurricane Season: Are We Prepared?" (http://hsc.house.gov/hearings/index.asp?ID=47) -- that FEMA still has not completed its updated federal disaster plan, drawing fire from some lawmakers, USA Today reported Chairman Bennie Thompson, D-Miss., called the delay "very disturbing" and said, "FEMA will have a lot of explaining to do if it is not ready when a hurricane makes landfall this season."

William Jenkins, director of homeland security issues with the Government Accountability Office, also testified (http://www.gao.gov/docsearch/abstract.php?rptno=GAO-07835T) to problems with FEMA's readiness for another major storm. He pointed to questions about the working relationships between the Federal Coordinating Officers, who make mission assignments to federal agencies for response and recovery in regions at risk for hurricanes, and Principal Federal Officials, who provide "situational awareness" to the Homeland Security secretary. As he summarized: It is critically important that the authorities, roles, and responsibilities of these designated FCOs and PFOs be clear and clearly understood by all. There is still some question among state and local first responders about the need for both positions and how they will work together in disaster response.

In addition, Jenkins expressed worries about the status of various FEMA efforts to address situational assessments, emergency communications, evacuations, search and rescue, logistics, and mass care and sheltering:

In various meetings with us and in congressional testimonies, FEMA has described a number of initiatives to address identified deficiencies in each of these areas and progress is being made on these multi-year efforts. However, none of these initiatives appear to have been tested on a scale that reasonably simulates the conditions and demand they would face following a major or catastrophic disaster. During the hearing, lawmakers also repeatedly voiced concerns about whether a National Guard stretched by war-zone deployments had enough resources to respond to natural disasters. Paulison told the committee, "We are going to prepare for whatever storm comes our way with what we have."

But some governors say what they have might not be enough in a big storm. Speaking during a telephone news conference held Monday, North Carolina Gov. Mike Easley warned that the Iraq war has depleted his state National Guard's fleet of vehicles, communications equipment and other gear, the Raleigh News & Observer reported (http://www.newsobserver.com/114/story/574010.html). Easley said there was enough equipment to handle hurricanes up to Category 3, but the state could find itself without adequate resources to handle a bigger storm or what he called a "no-notice" disaster. Other states that have also raised concerns about shortages of Guard equipment include Florida, Arkansas, Illinois and California, according to the Sarasota Herald Tribune (http://www.heraldtribune.com/apps/pbcs. dll/article?AID=/20070517/NEWS/705170305). In addition, Kansas Gov. Kathleen Sebelius complained that shortages of equipment and well-trained personnel impeded the Guard's response to tornadoes that recently hit her state.

This does not bode well for those of us facing a potentially fierce hurricane season -- and especially not for those of us who are still struggling to recover from past storms.

Monday, May 07, 2007

Gulf Watch: Serious weaknesses found in repaired New Orleans levees

(http://southernstudies.org/facingsouth/2007/05/seriousweaknesses-
found-in-repaired.asp)

With hurricane season less than a month away, experts from the United States and the Netherlands say flaws in New Orleans' repaired levee system could leave the region vulnerable to another disastrous breach like the one that occurred after Hurricane Katrina, which was the largest civil engineering disaster in U.S. history. So warns a special report from National Geographic (http://magma.nationalgeographic.com/ngm/levees/), which had Robert Bea (http://www.ce.berkeley.edu/~bea/about.html), a University of California at Berkeley engineering professor and former chief engineer for Shell Oil Co., inspect the protective barriers. Bea found multiple weak spots in critical areas, according to the magazine:

The most serious flaws turned up in the rebuilt levees along the Mississippi River Gulf Outlet ship channel, which broke in more than 20 places when Katrina's storm surge pounded it, leading to devastating flooding in the Lower Ninth Ward and St. Bernard Parish. Bea found several areas where rainstorms have already eroded the newly rebuilt levees, particularly where they consist of a core of sandy and muddy soils topped with a cap of Mississippi clay. "It's like icing on the top of angel food cake," Bea says. "These levees will not be here if you put a Katrina surge against them."

Bea also found that decade-old gaps remain in the floodwalls lining the Orleans Avenue Canal, and hurricane-damaged sections of the walls along the London Avenue and 17th Street Canals have not been repaired or replaced. Even more troubling, water appears to be seeping under the stout new floodwall erected along the Industrial Canal to protect the Lower Ninth Ward. The new wall sits atop steel sheet piles driven 20 feet into the ground, but water from holes in the canal bed, excavated before Katrina or scoured by the storm, may be seeping under the barrier through permeable layers of sand and silt.

Bea, who actually tasted the seepage to make sure it was brackish -- a sign that it was coming from the canal -- says the wall could fail in the next hurricane.

Bea helped lead a team of Berkeley experts that investigated the Katrina levee failures, and he's currently serving as an expert witness in a class-action lawsuit against the Army Corps of Engineers (http://www.leveelaw.com/). But he's not the only engineer who sees problems in the repaired structures. National Geographic also spoke with a Dutch engineer who recently inspected some of the city's new floodgates and pumps. The engineer, who asked to remain anonymous since he sometimes works with the corps, says that in the next big storm the structures may be "doomed to fail" as the gates lack any mechanism to remove debris that could keep them from closing in advance of a storm. The corps is currently depending on divers to clear obstructions.

Another problem plaguing the protective system are the pumps that the corps installed to carry rainwater out of the city; they vibrated excessively and had to be repaired. While the corps claims they're now working fine, other experts charge that they haven't been fully tested. Also casting a shadow of doubt over the pumps is the fact that the deal to provide them went to Moving Water Industries, a politically connected Florida firm that's currently the target of a Department of Justice lawsuit over corruption allegations. As we reported (http://southernstudies. org/facingsouth/2007/05/was-bid-for-neworleans-drainage-pumps. asp) last week, both the corps itself and the Government Accountability Office began investigating whether there were any improprieties in the awarding of that contract after it was discovered that the corps lifted the specs for the job directly from MWI's catalog.

Another expert pointing to flaws in New Orleans' levees is Ivor van Heerden of Louisiana State University's Hurricane Center (http://www.hurricane.lsu.edu/); he led a team of state experts that probed the levee failures and is another expert witness in the class-action lawsuit against the corps. Van Heerden agrees with Bea's evaluation of weak spots and also notes that a section of floodwall along the Duncan Canal in Jefferson Parish on the city's west side is in trouble, telling National Geographic:

"There is 1,900 feet of I-wall that actually dips -- sinking from its own weight," he says. Sheet pilings installed by the corps to shore up the weak wall may not be adequate, he says.

The New York Times reports (http://www.nytimes.com/2007/05/07/us/07levees.html) that U.S. Sen. Mary Landrieu (D-La.) has been informed of the apparent problems with the levees and floodwalls and plans to send a letter to the corps commander, Lt. Gen. Carl Strock, asking whether his agency's repair work was adequate.

Ensuring that the system protecting New Orleans from deadly flooding is especially critical now, with a more-intense-than-usual storm season anticipated. The hurricane prediction experts at Colorado State University (http://hurricane.atmos.colostate.edu/) last month said (http://hurricane.atmos.colostate.edu/ Forecasts/2007/april2007/) they expect a "very active" tropical storm season for 2007, with about nine hurricanes and 17 named storms. They estimate the probability of a major hurricane hitting the Gulf Coast at 49 percent, compared to last century's average of 30 percent.

Gulf Watch: New Orleans' economy improves, but infrastructure remains a disaster

(http://southernstudies.org/facingsouth/2007/04/new-orleanseconomy-improves-but.asp)

Nineteen months after Hurricane Katrina hit the U.S. Gulf Coast, New Orleans "may have turned a corner," concludes the latest Katrina Index (http://www.gnocdc.org/KI/KatrinaIndex.pdf) from the Greater New Orleans Data Center (http://www.gnocdc.org/) in collaboration with the Brookings Institution (http://www.brookings.edu/).

To justify its optimism, the index points to several bits of good news. They include the fact that newly hired "recovery czar" Ed Blakely -- who last week came under fire (http://www.wdsu.com/news/11826385/detail.html) for remarks (http://www.nytimes.com/2007/04/10/us/10orleans.html?ex=1333857600&en=c97051276da3621c&ei=5089&partner=rs syahoo&e mc=rss) in which he referred to the city's residents as "buffoons," likened its racial divisions to "the Shiites and the Sunnis," and said that those demanding the "right of return" are "using people" for political ends -- is pushing forward with a $1.1 billion recovery plan that emphasizes the redevelopment of commercial corridors in 17 areas of the city in hopes of attracting homeowners and stabilizing neighborhoods. Construction could begin as early as this September.

In addition, the number of unemployment claims are down significantly, with only 46 from New Orleans and 204 across the entire metropolitan area. At the same time, unemployment rates are 4 percent in New Orleans and 3.8 percent across the metro area -- well below the national rate of 4.5 percent in February. But other figures show that hard times still linger in the Big Easy -- especially for residents of modest means who rely on public amenities like schools, transportation and libraries:

* While one more public school opened in New Orleans this past month, 75 of the parish's public schools remain shuttered. In all, only 45 percent of New Orleans public schools operating pre-Katrina are open today, a figure that's inched up by only 4 percentage points since last September.

* Recovery of public transit remains stuck, with less than half of all routes open in New Orleans. Only 17 percent of pre-Katrina buses are operating in the city -- a figure that remains unchanged since March of 2006.

* The number of open state-licensed hospitals in the city remains frozen at 52 percent of pre-Katrina levels -- a number that has not budged in the past five months. Meanwhile, there are still no state-licensed hospitals open in neighboring St. Bernard Parish.

* Only 62 percent of public libraries that were open before Katrina are open today in New Orleans. That figure has not changed since June of 2006.

* Another child care center opened this past month in Orleans Parish, but 191 remain closed. In all, only 32 percent of the number of child care centers operating pre-Katrina are open today.

We would like nothing more than to see New Orleans turn a corner down the path to a full and just recovery. But we remain skeptical that the city has reached that corner yet.

Gulf Watch: Time is running out for Louisiana's vanishing coast

(http://southernstudies.org/facingsouth/2007/03/time-is-runningout-for-louisianas.asp)

Humans have no more than a decade left to act before the ongoing loss of Louisiana's coastline becomes irreversible. So conclude the experts in the first installment (http://www.nola.com/speced/lastchance/tp/index.ssf?/speced/lastchance/articles/day1.html) of a multipart series on coastal land loss (http://www.nola.com/speced/lastchance/) that the New Orleans Times-Picayune began running yesterday:

Unless, within 10 years, the state begins creating more wetlands than it is losing -- a task that will require billions of dollars in complex and politically sensitive projects -- scientists said a series of catastrophes could begin to unfold over the next decade.

These catastrophes would include Gulf waves breaking over suburban lawns, the forced abandonment of many outlying communities, the intensified battering of the nation's energy infrastructure, complete inundation of levees built to withstand only brief storm surges, and south-approaching tropical storms slamming into the city of New Orleans as though it were beachfront property.

The impact would hardly be limited to Louisiana, the paper warns:

The entire nation would reel from the losses. The state's coastal wetlands, the largest in the continental United States, nourish huge industries that serve all Americans, not just residents of southeastern Louisiana. Twenty-seven percent of America's oil and 30 percent of its gas travels through the state's coast, serving half of the nation's refinery capacity, an infrastructure that few other states would welcome and that would take years to relocate. Ports along the Mississippi River, including the giant Port of New Orleans and the Port of South Louisiana in LaPlace, handle 56 percent of the nation's grain shipments. And the estuaries now rapidly turning to open water produce half of the nation's wild shrimp crop and about a third of its oysters and blue claw crabs. Studies show destruction of the wetlands protecting the infrastructure serving those industries would put $103 billion in assets at risk.

Unfortunately, while various coastal restoration initiatives have been launched during the past 20 years, no project capable of reversing the loss is currently in line for approval, the paper reports.

As we noted in our report titled "A New Agenda for the Gulf" (http://www.southernstudies.org/NewAgendaGulf.pdf) released last week for the 18-month anniversary of Hurricane Katrina (a storm whose effects underscored the urgency of Louisiana's land-loss problem), a lack of federal leadership has impeded Gulf Coast reconstruction efforts. Inadequate action on Washington's part is also hampering coastal restoration, the Times-Picayune notes:

Congress provided a note of hope last year, voting the state a permanent 37.5 percent slice of offshore oil revenues for coastal restoration work. But full financing -- some $650 million annually -- won't kick in until 2017. During the critical next decade, the state will be receiving only about $20 million a year, a pittance in the face of a problem that will require tens of billions of dollars to solve.

If there's anything positive to be found in all this worrisome news, perhaps it's that Louisiana's coastal land-loss problem is finally getting the attention it deserves. Besides the Times-Picayune's series, Yahoo's Assignment Earth recently posted a piece (http://cosmos.bcst.yahoo.com/up/player/popup/?rn=49750&cl=1968560&ch=340958&src=news) about the problem, which it documented with the help of the folks at the Gulf Restoration Network (http://www.healthygulf.org/). But ultimately, reporting the problem is not going to fix it. Let's hope that these much-needed efforts to detail the land-loss crisis spark some decisive action before it's too late. http://southernstudies.org/facing-south/labels/Gulf%20Coast%20R econstruction%20Watch.asp

As a final reminder. Now that you know more about GoZones than you ever wanted to, the conclusions must be repeated. Never buy real estate investments based upon some short term benefit. You buy it, you own it. You can't move it and your tenants come from a 5 mile radius. Government benefits are self serving but YOU are not the one being served.

Chapter 12

Three Ways to Lose Money in Real Estate

Don't believe the hype. The more depressed that the real estate market gets, the more the promoters come out from under the woodwork, under their rocks, or wherever they have been hiding, to pitch their expensive—and unrealistic—plans and programs about how to get rich in real estate through foreclosures, probate purchases, and fixing and flipping. In this chapter, I want to share with you why the first two approaches make money for nobody but the people who run the seminars. Unless you're as handy at carpentry and plumbing as you are at pulling permits and using a calculator, fixing and flipping is another way to turn your savings into dust. I've been at this a long time—long enough to see countless well-intentioned people burned because they thought they could steal a bargain at foreclosure, identify a lucrative piece of property in a probate sale, or buy a fixer-upper, make it salable, and make a killing. These approaches simply don't work, and I want to show you why.

First let's talk about foreclosure. As I write these words, the residential real estate market is softening, which means that, sad to say, more families are losing their homes due to foreclosure. A lot of people have the idea that one man's loss is another man's gain. But when it comes to foreclosures, one man's loss may be the next man's loss, too. Why not buy foreclosed properties? The simple answer is that when you buy a house that's been foreclosed upon, you're buying a house that didn't sell. The owner of the house couldn't sell it and the bank couldn't sell it. They're just hoping that a sucker—I mean an "investor"—like you comes along, ready to take that white elephant off their hands. If a trained realtor couldn't make a good deal to sell the house, and if a bank which is surely more sophisticated about real estate than the average individual couldn't sell that house, then only somebody with a super-inflated ego or a highly erroneous belief in his own real estate selling skills could possibly imagine that he could do a better job.

Let's first consider what foreclosure is. Very simply, when an individual who owns a house, has taken out a mortgage on that house, and can no longer make the payments, there comes a time—and that time varies from state to state—that the bank is allowed to take possession of the house, put the owner out on the street, and then sell the house, using the proceeds to pay off what's left on the mortgage. Why do people end up in a situation where they risk foreclosure? Maybe they bit off more of a home loan than they could chew.

This happened all too often during the heyday of the sub-prime loan, when people were encouraged to buy far more house than they could afford. Who do you blame for that? You can certainly blame the lenders, because many of them acted unscrupulously in putting people into loans that their income could never have supported. But at the same time, people have to take responsibility for their own actions. We shouldn't be signing our names to documents—especially loan documents on a house where we are raising a family—unless we know exactly what is entailed in terms of how much we're borrowing and how much we owe.

All too often, home loans with interest only payments, or partial interest payments, or balloon payments, left homeowners in the precarious position of owing more—often far more—on their homes than the market price, especially in a down market like we are experiencing today. For whatever reason, though, people couldn't make the payments, they couldn't sell the house at a price that would allow them to pay off their mortgage, and the bank stepped in to recoup as much as it could of what turned out to be a very bad investment all around.

It's not as though a homeowner misses one payment and boom—the house is foreclosed and they're on the street. They must miss a few payments, and then burn through a grace period, again which varies from state to state, before a lender can foreclose on a house. During that grace period, also known as pre-foreclosure, a homeowner has the right to pay off the loan or make the account current. The homeowner can also hire a realtor or sell the property to a third party—but in a soft market—it's not always possible to get a good price. An owner can sell a property at public auction, but when you auction a house, there's no guarantee that the proceeds will be sufficient to pay off the mortgage. When none of these situations take place, the lender takes ownership of the property. Once this happens, the property becomes bank-owned or REO—real estate owned by a lender.

How do real estate investors try to make a buck in a situation like this? If a home is in pre-foreclosure, an investor can approach the homeowner and offer to buy the property. The good news for the owner is that he's out from under the mortgage and his credit rating doesn't suffer. The bad news is that he's also out of his house, and may have to sell the house at a steep discount, sometimes almost half of the actual value of the house. Investors can also look for public auctions of foreclosed properties. The problem here is that you don't have a lot of time to research the title or inspect the home, so you may be buying a lot of trouble along with the house. Who conducts the auction? It might be the bank, or if the property is government-owned, it might be a government agency like the Department of Veterans Affairs or the Department of Housing and Urban Development.

Investors who seek to buy properties in pre-foreclosure status can learn online which properties in their area of interest are in jeopardy of foreclosure. The smart ones will drive by a neighborhood repeatedly to get to know the house and its surroundings. Is it a desirable neighborhood? Up and coming or in decline? You can't tell that from a Web site. They'll also try to talk to the owner directly or find a neighbor who is in the know about the owner of the pre-foreclosure property. Information gathering also means determining, usually with a visit to the County Recorder's Office, how much the owner owes on the property and whether any other liens against the property exist. The folks who offer those expensive "get rich buying foreclosed properties" seminars will charge you a thousand bucks just to tell you to get that information; I'm including it here in the cost of the book.

If you've decided to go ahead and make an offer, strike while the iron is hot. You're not the only person out there looking for pre-foreclosure property, so before you speak to the owner, be ready to move. Have your own sense of what the property is worth and what you're prepared to pay for it, and make sure your financing is in order. Many people recommend contacting the owner in writing before you make a phone call or knock on his door with an offer. That's because the risk of foreclosure is not just a financial problem—it's an emotional and family problem as well. People who buy pre-foreclosure properties can be looked upon not as saviors but as vultures. You don't want to be in that position. But don't just contact the owner by mail once. You may need to do it repeatedly, until your timing matches with the buyer's timing for buying.

Do a walk-through of the property once you've gotten a basic agreement in place. If you're handy, and you can do your own repairs, that'll save you a fair amount of money. Then you need a contract to purchase the house, just as if you were buying a non-distressed property. You might be able to assume the loan, or loan terms available based on your credit may be better than anything the previous owner could have negotiated. If there are any other lien holders, meet with them—you might be able to negotiate a bargain. But before you finalize the deal, do a title search.

It all sounds great, right? But keep in mind that if you are going to buy a piece of property in pre-foreclosure, in an auction, or from the bank, you're still buying damaged goods. There you are, putting all this time, effort, trouble, and money—a *lot of money*—not to mention your own sweat equity if you're doing your own repairs—into a property that is more than likely to prove to be no bargain whatsoever. You think you're buying the house below market value—but what's the market value for a house that nobody wants? In a strong real estate market, and in a strong economy, there may only be a couple of foreclosures in a neighborhood at any given time. Right now, when the real estate market is sorting itself out from the sub-prime debacle, foreclosures abound. How do you find "market value" when no one knows how low the market is going to go? A house that feels like a "steal" in May could end up being an albatross in November. Ultimately, a house needs a couple or a family to move in, live there, and take care of it, or rent it out to someone else. If you are the "fortunate" investor able to seal the deal on a piece of pre-foreclosure property or a piece of property owned by a bank or an arm of the government, all this means is that you beat out the other speculators for the right to lose money on that house. More often than not, investments in foreclosed property turn out not to be lottery tickets but a path to bankruptcy. You might be willing to offer more than the other speculators, but what does that tell you? It means that all the other real estate investors in your neck of the woods were not willing to put down as much money on that property as you, in your infinite wisdom. It's too bad they already made a TV show called "The Biggest Loser," because that's how I would describe anybody unfortunate enough to offer the most money, out of all the speculators, to the owner of a foreclosure property. Once again, you've got to ask yourself whether you're smarter than all the other investors looking at foreclosures, *and* all the home buyers who passed up the opportunity to buy the house from a realtor or directly from the owner, *and* the bank or government entity currently in possession of the house. What do you know that they don't? What's in your crystal ball that allows you to predict that you can make money where others can't?

Do not be fooled by the name recognition of the seminar leaders or sponsors. Whether it's Donald Trump or the Author of Rich Dad, Poor Dad it does not change the results. If this sounds harsh, I'd rather you learn from me that foreclosures don't work than learning it in a hard and painful way, by going to the time, trouble, and expense of a property that costs you more in money and heartache than you could ever make if things really worked the way the foreclosure hucksters would like you to believe.

First, remember the process that the distressed homeowner goes through prior to foreclosure. At the first sign of trouble and while they still have a decent credit rating they will apply for an equity line of credit using their equity as security. The bank loved those loans for awhile. So, the homeowner, out of necessity, has already taken as much equity out of the property as they can. Then, when the money ran out and the payments kept going up they decided to put the house on the market before the foreclosure notices became a handicap on their ability to sell. Some houses actually sell during this period. The final step happens when the home doesn't sell and the owners don't keep their payments current. Because they have financial hardship they defer maintenance and create an attitude of "why repair the property when it's in foreclosure?" So, the Foreclosure is "a property that didn't sell" which means that it wasn't attractive at distressed prices so what are you going to do with it?

If you can't make money with foreclosures, and I don't believe that most people can, what about probate sales? Let's talk about the overall concept first. Probate is the process of ensuring that the estate of a deceased person is distributed in accordance with his will, that all debts and liens are paid off, and that everything goes according to Hoyle. Most people who possess considerable assets, whether real property or otherwise, establish trusts or other estate-planning mechanisms in order to make sure that their wills—and their property—don't get tied up in court, often for years, with expensive probate attorneys' meters turning.

But not everyone is that sophisticated, and it does happen that estates, often involving real property, end up in probate court.

And this is where probate buyers come in. The heirs to an estate, including real estate, often don't want the house, the farm, the apartment building, or the office building. They want cash—either to put in their own pockets or to pay off taxes or for some other purpose. The property may be located in a distant state, or it may not be something that two or more heirs could both make use of. So there are a lot of reasons why people in a probate situation would want to sell property.

The people who make money offering "training" in buying and selling probate properties would like you to believe that you can step in and buy at a discount of twenty to forty percent, or even more. They want to entice you into their seminars with the false promise that probate sellers are in such a hurry to dispose of property that they will do so for a steep discount. Forget it. Maybe that was true a generation ago, when folks might have been a little less sophisticated about investments. But there are two factors that mitigate against your ability to pick up a quick bargain from a probate sale. First, nobody's in that much of a hurry, or that stupid, to sell a piece of property worth $100,000 for only $60,000 or $70,000. They're just not going to do it. A lot of investing is based on the "greater fool" theory—you're willing to buy a property because you believe that at some point there will be a greater fool willing to pay more money to take it off your hands. Well, the greater fool in probate sales is the one who thinks that he's going to find a big bargain out there. It's just not going to happen.

In today's world, it's far too easy for owners of probate property to identify just how much a given piece of property is worth, thanks to the Internet. Often the probate attorney is required to get an appraisal on the property as well. It's also relatively easy for them to identify and engage a competent realtor in the area where that property is located, again thanks to the dissemination of information over the Web. Why should they sell to some person they find on the Internet whom they don't know, at a bargain, steep or otherwise, when they can conclude a transaction at market value just as easily? The simple answer is that they can't and they won't. There are few, if any, real bargains to be found via probate sales.

The second factor keeping you from getting rich quickly, slowly, or at medium speed through probate sales has to do with probate courts. These courts have a responsibility to the heirs to make sure that properties don't get sold in an undervalued way. The courts are simply not going to allow such a sale to take place. Again, why should they? The court might be in Wyoming and the property in question in Alabama, but a responsible realtor is just one phone call or e-mail away. Probate courts are simply not the gold mines for would-be real estate millionaires that the conniving seminar operators would like you to believe. The probate court will require an appraisal on any real property in the estate to calculate taxes due and to be sure that the heirs know the true value of the estate. The courts, as well as the state and federal taxing agencies, are also wise to the actions of some heirs who will sell inherited property at a loss to friends, neighbors or other relatives to lower their tax obligation on the estate. That trick has been discovered and may result in further penalties because of tax evasion. Be forewarned that the probate process is now pretty clean with full disclosure as required by law.

Finally, we turn to the idea of the fixer-upper. This has been a traditional path for making money in real estate, especially for those who are handy. The idea is that you locate a distressed piece of property in a decent or at least average neighborhood, buy it, fix it up so that it meets community or neighborhood standards and sell it at a nice profit. It sounds great…but I'm here to tell you that more often than not, you can put a lot of time and a lot of hard labor into a fix-and-flip and have nothing to show for it except a loss on your books. How could this be?

Simply put, when it comes to fixing and flipping, time is money. Starry-eyed newcomers to real estate typically underestimate the amount of time and money it will take to fix up the property. They also underestimate the amount of time it's going to take to find a buyer. At the same time, they overstate the amount of money they're going to earn when they finally sell the property. While they're busy underestimating and overestimating, the bank is busy collecting interest, because as I said, time is money. The longer it takes to sell the property, the smaller the profit and the greater the amount of money that the fixer-and-flipper will pay to the bank. This is also not by any stretch of the imagination a risk-free proposition. What if you buy a house today and the real estate market turns, so that you can't even recoup your initial investment when you come to sell the house? Or what if you knock out a wall in the house and discover, to your dismay, additional repair problems that are both expensive and time-consuming? To paraphrase Forrest Gump, a fixer-upper is like a box of chocolates—you never know what you're going to get. But the one thing you are not likely to get, I'm sad to say, is a profit. There are too many variables, too many uncertainties, and overall, too much market risk. Fixing and flipping, unfortunately, is not the path to real estate wealth for the novice or in many cases, the more experienced. But it might make a good T.V. show to entertain.

If this chapter has shattered your dreams of making a fortune in real estate, the way the seminar guys would like you to believe you can

(through foreclosures, probate sales, or fixing and flipping) then I've accomplished my mission. There are two ways to acquire knowledge. One is through your own experience, and the other is through the experience of other people. In this chapter, I've sought to offer you the sad experience of countless other people who thought that they could make money in real estate through these three methods. By and large, they didn't. But a new generation of hopeful investors arises every day, and the people with those full page ads for seminars on how to make money in these fields continue to prey on them. In this book, I've shown you a sensible, proven way of investing in real estate. That's the one way I know to make money. And now you've learned the three ways I know that almost certainly guarantee you heartache and loss. Can you still make a fortune in real estate? You bet.

Do it the right way, and you'll be very satisfied with your results. The way I've outlined in this book is a turn key approach that is disciplined but very effective. It is truly the Number 1 way to invest in the Number 1 investment in America which truly is real estate.

Chapter 13

Getting Moving

So far, we've talked all about real estate—how to find it, how to buy it, how to own and manage it. But now I want to talk about a topic even more important. That topic is *you*.

What good is knowledge if you don't have the mindset that permits you to put that information to use? I'm delighted to tell you that you now know everything you need to know in order to get **started** on the road to success with real estate, the greatest investment opportunity ever created. That's the good news. Everything that you've learned in this book will teach you how to move from financial worries to financial security…and ultimately, to financial freedom.

But knowing how to do something, and actually getting out there and doing it, are two entirely different things! Most people who are overweight know exactly what they need to do in order to achieve their dream weight. They know they need to eat less! They know they need to replace the high carb snacks with healthy choices. But the last time

I looked around, and I'm sure you've noticed the same thing…there are a lot of people out there who are carrying a few too many pounds around their waist! (Not to mention other places!)

So it's not enough to *know* how to succeed. It's also essential to have the thinking patterns that successful people employ, to make your dreams come true. In other words, your mind has to be working *with* you, and not *against* you, as you strive to reach new levels of financial success. And you cannot be afraid to fail. Remember, It is better to try and fail and not to try at all. Failure just leaves success for another day.

The Power of Thought

One of the greatest developments of the twentieth century in America was the concept of the motivational speaker, the motivational book, and the motivational class. Before Dale Carnegie became a worldwide organization, teaching people in every way of life how to succeed, there was just one person in a Philadelphia YMCA named Dale Carnegie teaching salespeople how to have a good attitude.

We also find Norman Vincent Peale publishing the first of his dozens of globally influential books, *The Power Of Positive Thinking*, and Napoleon Hill writing his success classic, *Think And Grow Rich*. Notice the similarity in the words of the two titles of these extremely influential books? That's right—it's *thinking*. It's not just what we *do* the counts. It's how we *think* about what we do that makes the difference.

It often happens that with any material of a self-help nature, all too many people buy the book (or the CD program or the videos) and never even open them or take them out of their shrink wrap. Others are more industrious—they'll actually make a start on reading or viewing the material. And then there are people like you— individuals who have the courage to read something new all the way to the end. By reading this far, you've demonstrated your commitment to creating a new financial life for yourself and for those you love. You now have most of the information you need. But what is your mind telling you about whether success in real estate can truly be yours? Are you getting positive or negative messages from your brain?

"I don't have enough money to get started."

That's not true — if you visit my website, www.TenPercentDown. com, you'll discover that getting started takes far less of an investment than you might have thought. And you've learned as much from this book already. "It's too late to make money in real estate—the boom has passed."

It might be too late for a monkey throwing darts at real estate classifieds tacked to a wall to make money. But for anybody who knows the true secrets of success, this is as advantageous a time as anyone could hope for. It's a great time to be investing in real estate…but you can only make that investment of your time, energy, and money, if you truly believe that you can succeed.

"Other people can get rich in real estate, but I won't be able to."

That statement is a perfect description of the power of negative thinking. If you believe you cannot, then you truly cannot. Let me share with you a poem that I wrote and had my children memorize:

You Are What You Think

If you think you are beaten, you are,

If you think that you dare not, you don't,

If you'd like to win but you think you can't,

It's almost certain you won't.

If you think you'll lose, you've lost,

For out in the world you'll find

Success begins with a fellow's will—

It's all in the state of mind.

If you think you are outclassed, you are;

You've got to think high to rise;

You've got to be sure of yourself before

You can ever win the prize.

Life's battles don't always go

To the stronger or fastest man;

But soon or late the man who wins

Is the man who thinks he **can**.

This advice is right on the money—it all comes down to attitude and belief in yourself. But how do you acquire that kind of positive approach to life, especially if you have not yet demonstrated to yourself and those around you the kind of financial success you deserve?

Rah-Rah Isn't Enough

The twentieth century answer was what I would today call rah-rah motivation. You know what I'm talking about. The speaker gets up on stage and makes you laugh, makes you cry, tells you great stories, has you believing in yourself, has you backslapping the fellow in the seat next to you, has you jumping up and down with enthusiasm! I know because I was one of them.

And then the audience goes home...and they forget all about it. The motivation was great while it lasted, but it had no long-lasting effects.

I ought to know. One of the many hats I've worn in my lengthy career has been that of motivational speaker! I actually had the privilege of sharing the podium with the likes of the Reverend Norman Vincent Peale, Cavett Roberts and many of the other great speakers and motivators of our time. I was able to rouse the audience to an emotional frenzy and have them ready to take on the world.

The only problem was that the next day, the world was back to its own habits of thinking negatively...and accomplishing very little.

So how *do* you succeed in a world where rah-rah motivation isn't enough?

Napoleon Hill, quoting Marcus Aurelius, wrote in *Think And Grow Rich*, "Anything the mind can conceive and believe...it can achieve." Well, that kind of thinking might have worked for the twentieth century. But here in the twenty-first, we've learned a critical lesson about ourselves. We aren't supermen and superwomen. We can't sprout wings and fly. We do have to live within our limitations, and one of the main limitations that affects so many of us...is fear.

Fear is a healthy response in situations where a genuine threat lurks. But the rest of the time, fear simply hinders us. How many individuals listen to my weekly radio program, have seen me speak, have read the material in this book, and said to themselves, "I know it will work, but I'm too afraid to move forward!" Usually the words are something like "but I'll start tomorrow" and then that tomorrow never comes because fear replaces action. An overwhelming majority of people feel that way, I'm sorry to say. *You* don't have to be one of them. Overcoming fear doesn't just mean walking over a bed of hot coals or otherwise demonstrating to yourself that you can handle situations that used to baffle you. It's about developing the quiet confidence that allows you to know that success will be yours.

The problem with statements like "Anything the mind can conceive and believe, it can achieve" is that they ignore another fundamental point that Napoleon Hill made in *Think And Grow Rich*. Motivation isn't enough. Positive thinking isn't enough. What you really need in order to succeed...is *a definite plan*. I dream about running a 4 minute mile but that goal will never be attained because I am way past my prime for that type of activity. Now an 8 minute mile is within reason. Setting unattainable goals is foolish. Setting attainable goals is wisdom.

You Now Have a Plan For Success

That's what you now have. The good news is that you now hold in your hands the plan you need, which if followed, will take you to the success you desire and deserve. You can think of everything you've read so far in this book as a recipe for success. Follow the recipe...and you'll get where you want to go. Mix things up in some other kind of combination...choose a different form of real estate in which to invest, buy it in a manner other than suggested here, manage it in ways that I don't recommend...and you won't be following the recipe. So you won't get the results. If, however, you're willing to try this recipe, I'm sure you'll be delighted with the results. Do what I do and you'll get the results that I get.

I like to cook and as a single father of 4 kids I was always selecting recipes that worked. I bought the 10 minute book for a healthy meal

And I often digested the books outlining the best meals for kids. Why would any parent waste time preparing meals that their kids wouldn't eat? One rule to follow is the recipe itself. If I changed the recipe I changed the results and the taste. I bought the book because I wanted predictable results Well that's what you have in your hands now. You have a recipe for financial success. And since it is number 1 why would you spend time trying to change it. Why not follow my outline exactly as I outlined it and see if you get the same results as millions of other satisfied investors?

When I was starting out in business, I did not have the benefit of a "recipe for success" like this. I wasn't born to fame and fortune, and to be honest, there was nothing that you could point to in my childhood in Peoria, Illinois that pointed me toward greatness or a high level of success. Yes, I was born on the Fourth of July, and yes, like many kids, I had a paper route that taught me the basics of business, finance, and customer service. The early morning paper route for the Peoria Journal Star also taught me discipline as I had to get up very early **every** morning to be sure the paper was delivered before I returned home and went to school. But I didn't have a roadmap or a recipe for success. I just had an alarm clock to make sure I awoke on time. Even when the snow covered the ground or it was raining cats and dogs. I just had the proverbial School of Hard Knocks in which to enroll.

Quite the Resume!

After high school, I completed four years in the United States Marine Corps, during which time I grew physically, spiritually, and mentally. Toward the end of my career in the Marine Corps, I began to attend classes at Oceanside-Carlsbad Junior College. By that point, I wished I was a civilian instead of a Marine. That internal conflict led me to create the slogan to which I adhere to this day—"Don't give up—Today could be the day." I kept a plaque with that inscription in my locker, so that I could see it every morning and evening.

Here are some of the jobs I had along the way: carhop at Andy's Pig n' Whistle and Kramer's, two hot spots in early 1950s' Peoria. Bongo drummer in a local rock group called the "Spotlights" (they called me Bongo Charlie!). Digging trenches for sprinklers for a landscaping service. Developing pictures and making prints for the editors of weekly newspapers. Running my own weekly newspaper. Managing the Colfax Press in Gibson City, Illinois. And then starting my own business—a weekly publication in Normal, Illinois, home of Illinois State University, called the *Normal News*.

I never stopped thinking, *Today could be the day!* That optimistic frame of mind I had trained myself to accept, during the final year of my Marine Corps service, made the difference for me when I was running the *Normal News*. I ran the paper out of an eight-foot-wide mobile home located in a mobile home park. I paid $1800 for that mobile home—a hundred dollars down and forty dollars a month. There were many months when I didn't know where I was going to get my hands on that forty dollars in order to make the payments. My partner Ken Irwin and I survived for more than a year on just one meal a day…and a lot of determination. I learned what it meant to strive to survive.

I also understood that poverty in my pocket did not mean poverty in my mind. I knew I could grow intellectually by experiencing many different things related to responsible personal achievement—and I knew that financial security would eventually follow.

California, Here I Come!

Before long, I created an opportunity for myself to go out to Beverly Hills, California—a big step for a fellow from Peoria! There, I caught on with one of the major brokerage houses, and in the 1970s, I became one of the most successful professionals and investors in Southern California. I took the success I created there—for others as well as for myself—and turned it into the foundation of a real estate business which I have operated now for several decades. So I've been talking to you with the experience of one who has been through many "boom and bust" cycles and therefore knows where the real money is to be made. And when I talk about having the right mindset, I also know what I'm discussing, because if I hadn't had the right attitude, I would never have survived my early business challenges. That's what qualifies me to speak not just about the outer game of how to purchase, own, and manage real estate, but the inner game of mental success as well.

Ideas That Make The Difference

I want to share with you, in the remainder of this chapter, some of the key attitudes and ideas that have made the difference for me, back when I was a young ex-Marine finding my way in the working world and even today as I share my knowledge of wealth building through this book, through my radio show, through speaking engagements, and in many other ways. These ideas will help you develop the mindset that goes along with the plan for success you've found in this book.

The first important lesson I learned was when I took a Dale Carnegie sales course. I learned a lot more than just selling in that course. I discovered that a person like myself, with a limited education and no "connections" had no limits in terms of income potential. That was great news for me...and I hope it's great news for you, too, if you come from the same sort of background. When I took the course, I discovered that I could control my emotions and control my environment. One central theme from that course continues to rule my life—and it's this—*If you act enthusiastic, you will be enthusiastic.*

From the first day I heard that critical lesson, I decided to act enthusiastic. Many days, it is nothing more than an "act"—but other people don't know that! They believe I'm having a great day every day! I don't tell them I have my bad days, too. But on the rare occasion when I do have a bad day, I'm usually able to talk myself out of it. If I don't, it's my loss. If I do, it's my gain.

People like to associate with others who are enthusiastic because if some of it rubs off, they feel happier. If you believe in yourself to the point that you create a natural enthusiasm about your job, your family, your religion, and your life, you'll be admired and followed by others. People are truly looking for leaders and a sourpuss doesn't attract a following. So many other people haven't learned how to believe in themselves. They believe you know something they don't and they'll hang around you awhile looking for answers. They won't stay long enough to become friends with you...because they'll discover that what you have is a positive attitude and they won't feel comfortable with that discovery and they won't feel comfortable with you. You remind them of their potential, and that can be a place way out of their comfort zone.

If you are puzzled about the process of creating a positive attitude I offer this method. I discovered many years ago that I loved going to Maui, Hawaii for vacation and relaxation. Whenever the departure date was close my attitude and excitement increased. Many times I've used that mind set to improve my attitude. I pretend that I'm leaving tomorrow morning for Maui and my attitude and enthusiasm changes. I know that I am deceiving myself but it is a positive deception with good results. You may use a different mental image to focus on what works for you. Maybe it's a Friday night date with someone special or the excitement you had on the birth of your first child. Draw upon your own positive experiences and you'll see that you can control your attitude and your feelings. Try it…it works. I have coupled that attitude with an action that W. Clement Stone used at all of his talks. It was simple and that is the reason it was powerful. You couldn't forget it. He said, in a loud voice…"Do it NOW…Do it NOW" which simply means don't procrastinate.

Fear of Failure…and Success

Most of us would rather accept ourselves the way we are, with all of our shortcomings and unfulfilled dreams, than step out and swing for the fences. We're afraid to fail, and we're afraid to succeed. But those fears cannot be allowed to dictate your life, or your financial future. Act enthusiastically, and your enthusiasm will grow. Of course, I'd be remiss if I failed to point out the Greek root of the word enthusiasm is "en theos," the God within. Acting enthusiastically ultimately means getting in contact with the God-force within each of us. That force that wants us to do well, to succeed, and to have an abundant life. There's a high price to pay for staying in self-acceptance when we aren't even coming close to our potential. Enthusiasm is the missing step between potential and achievement. We are all made for a purpose and that purpose is not based upon failure. A member of the audience I was speaking to threw this out to me after my talk. He said, "Don't worry if you fail all the time as you can always serve as an pitiful example." That may be true but there's no honor in that.

Prepare for Change

When you change your attitude and start to place your hopes for achievement in yourself (instead of looking to others for success, or blaming others for your failure), you must begin to prepare yourself for change. Some changes occur because others around us won't change. There's a reason they say it's lonely at the top! That may be true for you in the beginning, because you may not be surrounded right now by people with the same sort of aspirations and dreams that you have. Actually, we all have those dreams. The difference is that you, unlike so many others, are actually willing to do what's necessary to make your dreams come true. And for that, by the way, I congratulate you.

Don't give up. Just find new friends and new environments— people and places that support your desire for success and growth. Seek success—don't wait for it to come to you. I discovered many years ago that poor people cannot show you how to make money. Also it's simple to understand that you want to deal with people who have money because you can't earn money by having poor people as customers. Go where *it* is. Seek out those you admire from afar and get a close-up view, and you will begin to see what you can do to enjoy the same sort of success they have. I developed a simple formula for success, as a result of reading many of the self-help and motivational books that line the bookstore shelves. (Again, it wasn't enough for me to buy those books—I actually had to read them in order to benefit from them!) My formula was simple to create but not so simple to implement. Here it is:

1. Set your goals.
2. Pay the price.
3. Don't give up.

The first step—setting your goals—seems to be the easiest. After all, everyone knows what they want, right? Actually, that's not true! Few people have any idea what they want to do with their lives, and so they let other people decide for them, and then they just take whatever they get. They take the job that's offered for the pay that's provided. Their whole attitude is, "What you got is what you want." That mindset is counter to the natural act of creation and growth.

As the expression goes, there are three kinds of people—those who watch things happen, those who make things happen, and those who ask, "What just happened!"

I'd rather be the kind of person who makes things happen, and I know you feel the same way. I need to know in advance what I want to do, so I'll be sure and do it. I even develop a timetable so I can tell if I'm on schedule or not. How will you know when you arrive if you don't know where you're going?

For most of us, the biggest obstacle is procrastination. As Tony Robbins says, "The best thing to do with procrastination…is put it off!" Seriously, I conquered procrastination, which is actually a five-syllable word for laziness, by setting priorities. Now, my priorities may conflict with other people's priorities—if I'm trying to accomplish my goals and they aren't. That's when I realize that procrastination is no more than *the act of failure before you begin.* If we surround ourselves with people who accept whatever life hands them, we start to think that that's all we deserve. That's no way for you to live, and the time to stop living that way is right **now**. It's better to have tried and failed than not to have tried at all. And trust me—if you're willing to try the process that I've outlined in this book, if you have the desire to follow the recipe—success will be yours. Don't be afraid of failure because even that can be a positive learning experience. Failure is the opportunity to experience success on another day.

Are You Willing to Pay the Price?

Not everyone wants to pay the price. This is true in relationships—witness the high number of divorces in our society. This is true in schools—just look at the dropout rates. And it's certainly true when it comes to business and financial success. You may have to give up your present job and the security (or the illusion of security) that goes with it. Maybe you'll have to sacrifice some time with friends or family in order to get your dream of real estate to become a reality. People complain that they don't have enough money but are not willing to get a better education or work two jobs. I remember advising people that to succeed they only had to work for a half day and it doesn't matter which 12 hours you choose.

If the sacrifice appears too great, you may quit before you've tasted the nectar of sweet accomplishment. My advice: *Don't give up.* It may be harder to start next time. Worst yet, there may never even be a next time. That's why "don't give up" is the third of the three maxims by which I live my life, and which I humbly offer as a suggestion for you. The moment you give up may be the day before the greatest experience in your life. How do you know? As the expression goes, "Don't quit five minutes before the miracle!" How important is your self-respect, your dreams, your desire for a better life for yourself and your family? What will change if you don't? How will your decision to quit affect the rest of your life? Can you afford to pay the price of quitting? What kind of example are you setting for your family.

Thanks to my own success in real estate, I can afford a lot of things. But the one thing I could never afford is the price of quitting. Actually, I'll win every time, because my daily slogan is "Don't give up—today could be the day!" I believe it with my whole being and I've proven beyond any of my own doubts that it is not foolishness but a statement of faith within me. Indeed, I am the best judge of myself and my capabilities, and I know that you are the best judge of yourself. I also know that God has a plan for my life and "it's a plan for good not for evil."

Why do I believe in myself? I believe in me because I know He created me to be something special, just as He made you to be something special. I'm doing what I can with the talents I've been given, and I'll never stop searching for new goals. I believe in the slogan "By Example Shall You Lead." As an example, you can never forget the responsibility. You'll never want to.

We need to be alert to the negative influences in our lives that could influence us to be less than we *can* be. These negative influences sometimes come packaged as friends and relatives. Recognize them and work around them. Bad advice will go away...if good advice is encouraged to stay. Don't be like the poor man who sold hot dogs by the side of the road. Let me share his story with you now.

"The Man Who Sold Hot Dogs"

Many years ago there was a man who lived by the side of
the road and sold hot dogs.

He was hard of hearing so he had no radio.

He had trouble with his eyes so he read no newspaper.

But he sold hot dogs.

He put up signs on the highway telling how good they were.

He stood on the side of the road and cried: "Buy a hot dog,
Mister ?"

And people bought, because he was so enthusiastic.

He increased his meat and bun orders.

He bought a bigger stove to take care of his growing trade.

He was so happy selling hot dogs, and people enjoyed doing
business with him.

He finally got his son home from college to help him out.

But then something happened.

His son said, "Father, haven't you been listening to the
radio? Haven't you been reading the newspaper?

There's a recession.

The world situation is terrible

The domestic situation is worse."

Whereupon the father thought, "Well, my son's been to
college, he reads the newspaper, he listens to the radio, and
he ought to know."

So the father cut down on his meat and bun orders, he took down all his advertising signs, and no longer bothered to stand on the highway to sell his hot dogs.

And his hot dog sales fell, almost overnight.

"You're right, son," the father said to the boy.

"You're right."

Time to Get G.R.E.E.D.Y.!

So don't accept advice from someone who doesn't know! It's time to ask yourself whether you are a dreamer or a doer. Dreamers dream about the job they'd love to have, the person they'd love to marry, the place they'd like to visit or the knowledge they'd like to possess. The doer is the one who *does it now.* If you want to know how to be a doer, then I'd like you to consider my final piece of advice: It's time to get G.R.E.E.D.Y.

To be successful you've got to be G.R.E.E.D.Y. I'm not talking about the dictionary definition of greedy, which means "excessively eager for acquisition or gain"—thank you Funk & Wagnalls! Instead, when I say G.R.E.E.D.Y., I'm talking about an acronym for the basic ingredients of success. Remember Gordon Gekko in the 1980s' movie *Wall Street*? He said that "greed is good," but by greed, he meant selfishness. I'm not talking about greed that takes from others or has you compromising your integrity or morals. Instead, I'm talking about a whole new concept of being G.R.E.E.D.Y.—and here it is.

The first letter, G, represents the need for GOALS. It's tough to reach your destination if you haven't figured out where you're going. In order to be worthy of constant attention, though, a goal needs to be realistic and it requires your commitment to it. You shouldn't need a "stack of Bibles" on which to swear that you're going to stick to your goal, if it's important enough to you.

Take a little time and perform some self-evaluation. You'll come up with a reasonable list of worthy goals— write them down and review them constantly. Should any goal become unrealistic, cross it off or replace it with another.

The R in G.R.E.E.D.Y. stands for RESPONSIBILITY. You are responsible for your actions, for the sum total of what you are. You are therefore responsible enough to recognize your own personal accountability. Your goals become your personal responsibility. They are your personal blueprint for success. You must accept responsibility for your decisions and directions, your reaction to others, and your environment.

To be responsible means, above all else, understanding your responsibility to yourself. As a decision-making, free-thinking person, you constantly program your habits, actions, and reactions. Should you be dissatisfied with the results you're receiving, it's your duty as a responsible person to change those results by changing your actions. Although abrupt changes are highly unlikely, small, subtle changes and corrections applied with consistency will change habits, actions, and reactions. A responsible person does not blame others for his or her own failure, but rather adapts to the influence of others and continues to follow his or her own course of action. Create your goals…and be responsible for their fulfillment.

The next letter E is for EXPERIENCE. There are two kinds of experience in the world—yours and that of other people. Through the process of formal education, we learn from the experiences and accumulated knowledge of others. From our parents and friends we acquire a broad range of advice and practical knowledge. We either accept or reject that wisdom, depending on our mood. We can also have "subconscious experience," which we acquire while dreaming or through self-hypnosis. This type of experience is still yours, because your subconscious cannot tell the difference between a real or imagined experience, so the results are the same. In other words, whatever you tell yourself, you're going to believe. If you tell yourself that you have a great chance of success, you probably will. If you tell yourself you have a great chance of failure then you probably won't even start.

Keep in mind also that it's a lot cheaper to acquire the experience of other people than to have to spend years of trial and error finding out something for yourself. That's why I'm strongly suggesting that you piggyback on the decades of experience I have in the financial world, and especially with regard to real estate, because the experience I've got can make your dreams come true but avoiding the mistakes that hinder your progress.

So *you* set goals, *you* are responsible for their fruition, and *you* are constantly learning, through your own experience and the experience of others.

This takes us to our fourth letter—the letter E for ENTHUSIASM. We've already talked a lot about the importance of enthusiasm, so it won't surprise you that I'm offering it here as a key to success. Enthusiasm is the thermometer by which others measure your commitment to yourself and your goals. If you don't believe in yourself, it will show in your lack of enthusiasm. Try selling your ideas to someone without enthusiasm, and see what happens. Try selling anything to anybody without enthusiasm and you'll be missing one of your most vital selling tools. Despite all the product knowledge I could muster, I would hate to sell against someone who is fired with enthusiasm, because it is contagious!

I mentioned earlier the lesson I learned at Dale Carnegie—if I act enthusiastic, I'll be enthusiastic. It works.

It pays big dividends. Few people want to hang around a sourpuss. By contrast, everyone enjoys the company of an enthusiastic person. Enthusiasm will get you through tough times, dreary days, setbacks, and the negative opinions of others. Get in touch with the God within—that's what enthusiasm is all about.

So now you've got goals, you understand your responsibility for creating your own life, you're learning from your own experience and that of others, and you're living with enthusiasm. This takes us to the letter D, which stands for...DETERMINATION. Upon the rock of determination is built the foundation for all progress. Without the ability to see things through to the very end, great dreams have crumbled and ideas have been buried along with their creator.

Regardless of our place in life, we all have our dreams and desires. Those who quit before they achieve success are no better than those who never tried, because the results are the same. It's that old cliché, winners never quit, and quitters never win. Many times, the winner is nothing more than the person with the most determination.

We all have different talents and goals. But we all have one common commodity—time. How we use it and the extent to which we use it determines our results as surely as our ability. If you spend an hour doing a job that requires two hours and quit with the job half done, you've wasted an hour. But take three hours to do the job the right way, and you've used all of the time the best way you could.

It's been said about time that we can win a million dollars in the lottery, but not a million hours, and that the rich person and the poor person have exactly the same number of hours in a day. It really comes down to what use we make of the hours allotted to us. If we set goals, if we recognize our responsibility for the way our lives unfold, because of the effort we take, if we are gaining experience (our own and that of others), if we are acting enthusiastically, and if we demonstrate through determination, that takes us to the final letter in the word G.R.E.E.D.Y.—Y for YOU.

Without *you*, where would you be? Think about it— *you* make everything happen. *You* set the goals, accept the responsibility, create the experience, fuel the enthusiasm, and control the determination, so that your unique creative power can aspire to greatness never before imagined. You are the center of your universe, the creation of God's unlimited ability. Your limits are self-imposed—no one can put limits on you. So that's what being G.R.E.E.D.Y., at least in my mind, is all about!

If we have a common fault, it is that we fail to realize our true potential. How often do we react in ways that can only be described as primitive to challenges and perceived threats that, in the cold light of reason, turn out to be far less important than we initially imagined. We need to know how to succeed outwardly, which has been the focus of the previous chapters of this book. At the same time, we need to know how to create inward success, which has been my mission in this critically important final chapter. In this book, you have found the action steps necessary to create the success in real estate that you deserve. In this chapter, you have found the method for creating the plan of action that will allow your success to develop.

Body, Mind, and Spirit

We live in an era when more and more of us are recognizing that our lives comprise partnerships among our body, our mind, and our spirit. We've got to take the best possible care of ourselves physically in order to have the energy to do what we want to do. We have to feed our minds properly—give them the right nutrition, in the form of intelligent motivation (as opposed to that rah-rah motivation we were talking about earlier), so that our minds are working with us and not against us. And we must also recognize the spiritual source of all that is good, God who presides over this world and wants the best for us, the same way we want the best for our children. As you read this my next book will be available entitled "Living a Balanced Life, Body, Mind and Spirit." Look for it as your strive for financial and emotional stability.

Motivation in the twenty-first century is all about achieving a balance among body, mind, and spirit, and this is an area to which I intend to devote much time and thought in writings, on my radio program, and on the Internet. For now, I can share with you this incontrovertible fact: Success goes to the person who recognizes that great things will come to us if we work hard for them. I hope you'll work hard, that you won't be one of the people who give up before they even start, and that you'll follow this recipe that I've been privileged to provide with you here. But before we go, I want to share with you a few thoughts about the world in which we live.

The Greatest Threat

The greatest threat to the American way of life comes from the world of radical Islam, which demonstrates on a daily basis, around the world, its absolute hatred for everything that we consider precious— our freedoms, our modes of religious expression, and our political system. Nothing in my lifetime has ever come close to matching the scourge that radical Islam represents, both in this country and around the world. It has been said that only one-tenth of the world's Muslims are radicalized and support the sort of terror that Osama Bin Laden and others have perpetrated. If there are 1.5 billion Muslim's in the world, this means that we are talking about 150 million radicals.

But if Islam is indeed a religion of peace, why aren't the other 1.35 billion Muslim's speaking out courageously against their radical brethren? Where are the so-called "moderate" Muslims? Their almost universal failure to castigate, criticize, and condemn the radical ten percent leads to the question of whether they secretly support the aims and the means of radical Islam. Are the so-called "moderates" hiding behind a fig leaf of pretending to be opposed to the radicals? Or does their very silence make them complicit in the dastardly work of the radical Islamists? I personally have some Muslim friends and I know they hate the actions of those who kill in the name of Allah or jihad.

People say to me, "Don't dare criticize the Muslims. They'll kill you and your family." I doubt it. People have always had to speak truth in order to preserve power, and that is what I am doing. I would like to direct you to my Web site, www.MessageForMuslims.com, for a broader treatment of this issue. As a Christian, I consider this threat too real to ignore. None of us can minimize the importance of this threat, so please take a moment to view that Web site and learn about what you can do. I would like my Message to Muslims printed in full page ads in major newspapers everywhere. I would like to alert every Jew and Christian to the real threat that we are leaving for our children to deal with. I also want to alert every Muslim that their religion has been hijacked and it is up to them to do something about it.

Until they do, they will be aligned with terrorist, murderers and killers whose destiny is to die by the methods they impose on others. The choice couldn't be clearer and it's time to recognize it.

Chapter 14

Real Estate Performance History

PART ONE: MEDIAN HOME VALUES

Median home values adjusted for inflation nearly quadrupled over the 60-year period since the first housing census in 1940. The median value of single-family homes in the United States rose from $30,600 in 1940 to $119,600 in 2000, after adjusting or inflation (see graph). Median home value increased in each decade of this 60-year period, rising fastest (43 percent) in the 1970s and slowest (8.2 percent) in the 1980s. Both home values adjusted and unadjusted for inflation are presented. These values refer to owner-occupied single-family housing units on less than 10 acres without a business or medical office on the property.

Median Home Values—Adjusted to 2000 dollars

2000	1990	1980	1970	1960
$119,600	$101,100	$93,400	$65,300	$58,600

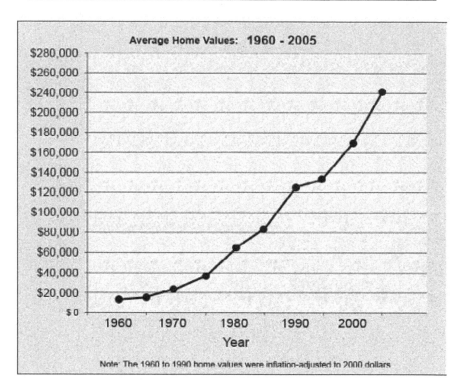

To adjust for inflation, the 1940 to 1990 median home values were adjusted to 2000 dollars using the appropriate CPI-U-RS adjustment factor.

Median Home Values: Unadjusted 216

2000	1990	1980	1970	1960
$119,600	$79,100	$47,200	$17,000	$11,900

Source:http://www.census.gov/hhes/www/housing/census/
histcensushsg.html
http://www.census.gov/const/C25Ann/soldmedavgprice.pdf

Median Home Values

Median home values adjusted for inflation nearly quadrupled over the 60-year period since the first housing census in 1940. The median value of single-family homes in the United States rose from $30,600 in 1940 to $119,600 in 2000, after adjusting for inflation (see graph). Median home value increased in each decade of this 60-year period, rising fastest (43 percent) in the 1970s and slowest (8.2 percent) in the 1980s. These values refer to owner-occupied single-family housing units on less than 10 acres without a business or medical office on the property.

Median Home Values: Unadjusted

2000	1990	1980	1970	1960
$119,600	$79,100	$47,200	$17,000	$11,900

Source:http://www.census.gov/hhes/www/housing/census/histcensushsg.html
http://www.census.gov/const/C25Ann/soldmedavgprice.pdf

Census bureau Median and Average Sales Prices of New One-Family Houses sold

New single family home costs:
1960: $16,500
1965: $18,900
1970: $23,400
1975: $39,300
1980: $64,600
1985: $84,300
1990: $122,900
1995: $133,900
2000: $169,000
2005: $240,900

Home prices source:
http://www.huduser.org/periodicals/ushmc/summer02/toc.htm

Chapter 15

Get Out of Stocks Now!!!

March, 2008 Newsletter
By Chuck Salisbury, MBA

I'm still concerned about all the retirement account money that's invested in the stock market. As a former stockbroker with 22 years as a Top Producer at Smith Barney, Shearson and Prudential, I gave everyone a buy signal over 6 months ago because I believed the market was overpriced and would adjust because of the Sub Prime market collapses . I told everyone to liquidate any money that you had invested in the stock market. That included all Mutual Funds that may have all or a portion invested in U.S. Stocks. A few people took my advice and liquidated. They paid their taxes and invested in Real Estate. Without exception THEY are all happy. Those that didn't sell are biting the bullet. Perhaps the reason you didn't sell is because your stock broker told you a story about the coming rally, buying opportunities, DOW going to 15,000. or some other nonsense. Stockbrokers don't lie intentionally because they really don't have a clue what the market will do the next day. Nobody does. But they do know that they are judged by the amount of assets they have under management and they don't want to give up any client or any managed money.

Everyone has heard that Bear Sterns collapsed recently which signals further weakness in the Mortgage Banking Industry. Who will be next? Bad news comes in threes in the securities market. Remember Enron and then MCI Worldcom and then another cable network company called Adelphia.

So, if you didn't listen before I want EVERYONE to listen now. GET OUT and don't depend upon the opinions of your stockbroker or market guru's on the T.V. An example is a guy named Jim Kramer, national radio and T.V. host, who said, a week before the Bear Sterns collapse, not to worry about Bear Sterns because they were financially solid. He told investors to hold the stock. On Monday they were taken over at $2.00 a share after a federal bail-out. The stock formerly traded at $170.00 a year ago. Do not listen to those who earn money handling your money on a straight commission basis. They are motivated to tell you whatever to keep your money with them.

I truly want you to make money and not loose money. I tell everyone at my seminars this simple but powerful example. If you invested $100,000. in the stock market and it declined 50% you would have $50,000. left. To get even and to regain the $100,000. balance in your account, the remaining money would have to grow 100% . It is so much HARDER to regain your losses than to avoid them. So, whether it's Retirement Money or just Investment Money get out of the stock/mutual fund markets. And never look back as you increase your net worth and actually have appreciating assets to take care of you when you retire. Remember, real estate is the ONLY investment that keeps pace with inflation so that's where your retirement money needs to be.

Don't take a risk with your future. If you have any questions be sure and call us at 1-949-502-3335. Happy Investing.

One Final Request

I believe that success means recognizing the responsibility to give back to the world. Every so often a situation comes along that, at the time it occurs, is too terrible to ignore. But before long, it is swept away on the tide of current events and all too quickly forgotten. 9/11 was just such a tragedy for America. For me, the tragedy of Beslan, Russia is another such situation and I cannot ignore it, and I hope you won't, either.

The school hostage crisis in Beslan, in September 2004 in the Caucasus region of the Russian Federation, resulted in the death of 344 civilians, including 186 **children**. For me, the tragedy of Beslan—instigated by Muslim Chechen soldiers—is too great to ignore. I, along with others, am working to build a new church in that community, and I invite you to join me in supporting this vital effort.

I hope you'll take a moment to view our Web site, www. TheChildrenofBeslan.com. I want to create a visible symbol to represent the differences between Christ's love for everyone and the Muslim faith that validates the horrific events in September, 2004. Your support can positively influence the living while remembering those who were killed in the name of Allah.

Chapter 16

Reverse Mortgages

Many senior citizens are using reverse mortgages to supplement social security, meet unexpected medical expenses, make home improvements, and more. Your home is probably your largest single investment, so it is smart to know more about reverse mortgages and decide if one is right for you! I believe it's important to present my conclusion about this Government created program. I've concluded that a Reverse Mortgage is a seniors last desperate step before insolvency and that there is a **better** and **safer** method for accomplishing the objective which is to increase monthly income. With my guidance and instruction they can also increase their net worth rather than eliminate it. That being said, let's examine what a HUD created Reverse Mortgage is.

Exactly what is a reverse mortgage?

A reverse mortgage is a special type of loan used by senior citizens to convert the equity in their homes into more income. The money obtained through a reverse mortgage can provide senior citizens with the financial security they need to fully enjoy their retirement years.

What types are available?

There are three basic types:

- Single-purpose reverse mortgages, which are offered by some state and local government agencies and nonprofit organizations;

- Federally-insured reverse mortgages, which are known as Home Equity Conversion Mortgages (HECMs), these are backed by the U. S. Department of Housing and Urban Development (HUD); and

- Proprietary reverse mortgages, which are private loans that are backed by the companies that develop them.

How do you qualify?

To qualify for a reverse mortgage you must be at least 62 years old and own your home or condominium. There is no income or medical requirements to qualify.

What are the advantages?

The right reverse mortgage can enable a homeowner to maintain financial independence and an adequate standard of living. You retain ownership of the home and do not make monthly repayments because this will be made from the proceeds of the sale of the home.

What are the disadvantages?

Reverse mortgages have complex contract terms that are confusing and can greatly impact the overall cost. Borrowers may encounter numerous financial hazards. First, they tend to be very expensive when compared with a conventional mortgage.

Example:

A typical reverse mortgage may provide to the consumer a $300 per month payment with a monthly compounded interest rate of 12%. Over the course of ten years, they will receive $36,000, but by that time they will owe approximately $70,000-almost twice as much as they received.

The second disadvantage is the complex and confusing contracts that can have a tremendous impact on the overall cost to the borrower. The complexity of the contracts often allow lenders and third parties involved in arranging reverse mortgages to not fully disclose the loan's terms or fees. Numerous other front-end and/or back-end fees can also quickly drive up the costs. These fees can include origination fees, points, mortgage insurance premiums, closing costs, servicing fees, shared equity and shared appreciation fees.

Example:

One case involves a lawsuit filed by the San Mateo County Public Guardian which, on behalf of an 83-year old person, alleged that the lender unfairly and unconscionably charged what was in effect a shared appreciation fee. This fee gave the lender an automatic 50% interest in the difference between the base value of the home when the loan was signed and the appreciated value of the home when the loan terminated, even though the fee bore no relation to the amount actually borrowed.

Additionally, the cost of the reverse mortgage soared when this person was required to purchase an annuity in conjunction with the reverse mortgage. An annuity is an insurance product financed out of the home's equity to provide monthly payments to the borrower immediately or after a certain number of years.

The San Mateo County Public Guardian alleged that the lender charged this person the cost of the annuity immediately and that interest began compounding on that fee even though they were not due to receive any payment on the annuity until six years after the loan began, at age 89.

Under this arrangement, if the home owner had died before the six-year period ended, the estate would see no benefit from the annuity purchase, although it had been paid for in full.

What happens if you leave your home?

Reverse mortgages require that the home you take out the reverse mortgage on is your primary residence. In order to avoid having to repay your reverse mortgage, you cannot leave your home unoccupied for longer than a year -- 365 days. If you must go to a nursing home unexpectedly, and stay longer than 365 you will be required to repay your reverse mortgage.

Are there any special things you should know?

Lenders generally charge origination fees and other closing costs. Lenders may also charge servicing fees during the term of the mortgage. The lender usually sets these fees and costs.

The amount you owe grows over time. Interest is charged on the outstanding balance and added to the amount you owe each month. That means your total debt increases over time as payments are made to you and interest accrues.

Reverse mortgages:

- May have fixed or variable rates. Most have variable rates that are tied to a financial index and these are likely to change according to market conditions.

- Can use all or some of the equity in your home, leaving fewer assets for you and your heirs. A "no recourse" clause, found in most reverse mortgages, prevents either you or your estate from owing more than the value of your home when the loan is repaid.

Because you retain title to your home, you remain responsible for property taxes, insurance, utilities, fuel, maintenance, and other expenses. Interest on reverse mortgages is not deductible on income tax returns until the loan is paid off in part or whole.

There are 5 options on how you can receive payments

Type of option available	How option is paid
Tenure	Equal monthly payments as long as at least one borrower lives and continues to occupy the property as a principal residence.
Term	Equal monthly payments for a fixed period of time.
Line of credit	Unscheduled payments or installments, at times and amounts of your choosing until the line of credit is exhausted.
Modified tenure	Combination of line of credit with monthly payments for as long as you remain in the home.
Modified term	Combination of line of credit with monthly payments for a fixed period of months selected by you.

Life expediency charts are used to predict how a long a person will live. When you based this on the calculations for a reverse mortgage, monthly payments will be higher for the older individual because it calculated that they will be receiving payments for a shorter period of time.

Current Age	Projected Age	Estimate Years for Payment
65	84	19
70	85	15
75	86	12
80	89	9

This calculation is based on a single 65-year old person whose home is paid off.

Loan Calculations	Monthly Adjusting HECM	Annual Adjusting HECM	Fannie Mae HomeKeeper
Current interest rate index	4.99%	4.99%	5.30%
Current effective loan rate	**6.99%**	**8.59%**	**8.75%**
Growth rate in line-of-credit	7.22%	8.94%	0%
Cap on effective loan rate	16.99%	13.59%	20.75%
Value of your home	**$400,000**	**$400,000**	**$400,000**
Lending limit	$362,790	$362,790	$417,000
Lesser of limit or home value	$362,790	$362,790	$400,000
Loan principal limit	$249,237	$210,781	$193,140
Less loan fees to lender	$7,256	$7,256	$8,000
Less Mortgage Insurance	$7,256	$7,256	$0
Less other closing costs	$2,334	$2,334	$2,218
Less service fee set-aside	$3,947	$3,493	$3,401
Cash available to you	**$228,444**	**$190,442**	**$179,521**
Less liens on your home	$0	$0	$0
Less necessary repairs	$0	$0	$0
Less other upfront cash	$0	$0	$0
Less Desired line-of-credit	**$0**	**$0**	**$0**
Left for monthly advance	$228,444	$190,442	$179,521
Monthly advance: Tenure	**$1,736**	**$1,636**	**$1,583**
Plus no more mortgage payments	$0	$0	$0
Equals increase in monthly cash	**$1,736**	**$1,636**	**$1,583**

This calculation is based on a married couple 69-year old husband and 67 year old wife who still owe money on their home.

Loan Calculations	Monthly Adjusting HECM	Annual Adjusting HECM	Fannie Mae HomeKeepe
Current interest rate index	4.99%	4.99%	5.30%
Current effective loan rate	**6.99%**	**8.59%**	**8.75%**
Growth rate in line-of-credit	7.22%	8.94%	0%
Cap on effective loan rate	16.99%	13.59%	20.75%
Value of your home	**$400,000**	**$400,000**	**$400,000**
Lending limit	$362,790	$362,790	$417,000
Lesser of limit or home value	$362,790	$362,790	$400,000
Loan principal limit	$253,590	$216,223	$173,060
Less loan fees to lender	$7,256	$7,256	$8,000
Less Mortgage Insurance	$7,256	$7,256	$0
Less other closing costs	$2,913	$2,913	$2,676
Less service fee set-aside	$3,862	$3,432	$3,456
Cash available to you	**$232,303**	**$195,366**	**$158,928**
Less liens on your home	$50,000	$50,000	$50,000
Less necessary repairs	$0	$0	$0
Less other upfront cash	$0	$0	$0
Less Desired line-of-credit	**$0**	**$0**	**$0**
Left for monthly advance	$182,303	$145,366	$108,928
Monthly advance: Tenure	**$1,416**	**$1,271**	**$945**
Plus no more mortgage payments	$0	$0	$0
Equals increase in monthly cash	**$1,416**	**$1,271**	**$945**

This calculation is based on a single 69-year old person whose home is paid off.

Loan Calculations	Monthly Adjusting HECM	Annual Adjusting HECM	Fannie Mae HomeKeeper
Current interest rate index	4.99%	4.99%	5.30%
Current effective loan rate	**6.99%**	**8.59%**	**8.75%**
Growth rate in line-of-credit	7.22%	8.94%	0%
Cap on effective loan rate	16.99%	13.59%	20.75%
Value of your home	**$400,000**	**$400,000**	**$400,000**
Lending limit	$362,790	$362,790	$417,000
Lesser of limit or home value	$362,790	$362,790	$400,000
Loan principal limit	$262,297	$227,469	$214,180
Less loan fees to lender	$7,256	$7,256	$8,000
Less Mortgage Insurance	$7,256	$7,256	$0
Less other closing costs	$2,913	$2,913	$2,818
Less service fee set-aside	$3,674	$3,292	$3,279
Cash available to you	**$241,198**	**$206,752**	**$200,083**
Less liens on your home	$0	$0	$0
Less necessary repairs	$0	$0	$0
Less other upfront cash	$0	$0	$0
Less Desired line-of-credit	**$0**	**$0**	**$0**
Left for monthly advance	$241,198	$206,752	$200,083
Monthly advance: Tenure	**$1,969**	**$1,884**	**$1,831**
Plus no more mortgage payments	$0	$0	$0
Equals increase in monthly cash	**$1,969**	**$1,884**	**$1,831**

Our conclusion is that doing a Reverse Mortgage is the final step towards financial insolvency for many seniors. At **www. TenPercentDown.com** we show homeowners how to turn equity into income, preserve and increase their net worth and home equity and let their estate increase 10% a year or more while providing monthly income. The good news is you don't have to sell your house. It remains a part of your estate and the equity can continue to increase. Make an appointment with a Financial Consultant at our office if you are over 55 or retired and have a substantial equity in your home. We do have a better plan and you will not have to pay the excessive fees associated with a Reverse Mortgage. Call 949-910-6028 or 949-502-3335 and ask for Victor or Chuck for a phone appointment or in house meeting. Don't think about getting a reverse mortgage until you consider a better way that allows you to keep your home and actually increase your net worth.

America is in a Financial Crisis

KNOW 3 THINGS TO DO TO PROTECT YOUR ASSETS
AND GROW YOUR WEALTH

Chuck Salisbury knows Americans are scared about investing right now. That's because, as a veteran financial expert, he's spent decades developing successful strategies for wealth attainment as the markets have risen and fallen repeatedly.

In November 2007 Chuck wisely advised his clients to get out of the stock and mutual fund markets: a move that saved many of those who listened the money they will need to retire.

Today, Salisbury continues to advise those who consult with him to avoid these markets, and to avoid investing in annuities and precious metals because these investments do not keep pace with inflation.

Thanks to government-backed bailout plans, which have flooded the currency market with trillions of dollars, "we are headed for a super inflation period," says Chuck.

As investors YOU must know:

- What is the ONLY investment in America that keeps pace with inflation.
- You must also know how to protect your self against losses.
- You must understand why you cannot trust your broker or Financial Advisor to give you unbiased investment advice.

So why Chuck Salisbury? Because he has the experience and the integrity to offer conclusions that are the results of 40 years of investing in and building investment real state projects and managing money for clients of Prudential, Smith Barney and Shearson Lehman.

This combination of experience and research is yours for FREE as he doesn't invoice clients for his advice. "I just don't want people to make more mistakes" he says on radio and in his seminar. Your Free Bonus for buying this book is his 90-minute seminar. You can watch it by going to; www.TenPercentDown.com/bonus. Then you can register on his website for free and enjoy all the investment resources available to hundreds of thousands of serious investors looking to retire with enough money to provide a comfortable "Income for Life".

Chuck is Available for Radio and T.V. interviews nationwide by pre-arranged appointments. He can be reached by email at; Chuck@tenpercentdown.com or call 1-877-Ten-Down or 949-502-3335

BUY A SHARE OF THE FUTURE IN YOUR COMMUNITY

These certificates make great holiday, graduation and birthday gifts that can be personalized with the recipient's name. The cost of one S.H.A.R.E. or one square foot is $54.17. The personalized certificate is suitable for framing and will state the number of shares purchased and the amount of each share, as well as the recipient's name. The home that you participate in "building" will last for many years and will continue to grow in value.

Here is a sample SHARE certificate:

YES, I WOULD LIKE TO HELP!

I support the work that Habitat for Humanity does and I want to be part of the excitement! As a donor, I will receive periodic updates on your construction activities but, more importantly, I know my gift will help a family in our community realize the dream of homeownership. **I would like to SHARE in your efforts against substandard housing in my community!** *(Please print below)*

PLEASE SEND ME _____ SHARES at $54.17 EACH = $ $_____

In Honor Of: _____

Occasion: (Circle One)   HOLIDAY   BIRTHDAY   ANNIVERSARY

        OTHER: _____

Address of Recipient: _____

Gift From: _____ *Donor Address:* _____

Donor Email: _____

I AM ENCLOSING A CHECK FOR $ $_____ PAYABLE TO HABITAT FOR HUMANITY <u>OR</u> PLEASE CHARGE MY VISA OR MASTERCARD *(CIRCLE ONE)*

Card Number _____ Expiration Date: _____

Name as it appears on Credit Card _____ Charge Amount $ _____

Signature _____

Billing Address _____

Telephone # Day _____ Eve _____

PLEASE NOTE: Your contribution is tax-deductible to the fullest extent allowed by law.
Habitat for Humanity • P.O. Box 1443 • Newport News, VA 23601 • 757-596-5553
www.HelpHabitatforHumanity.org